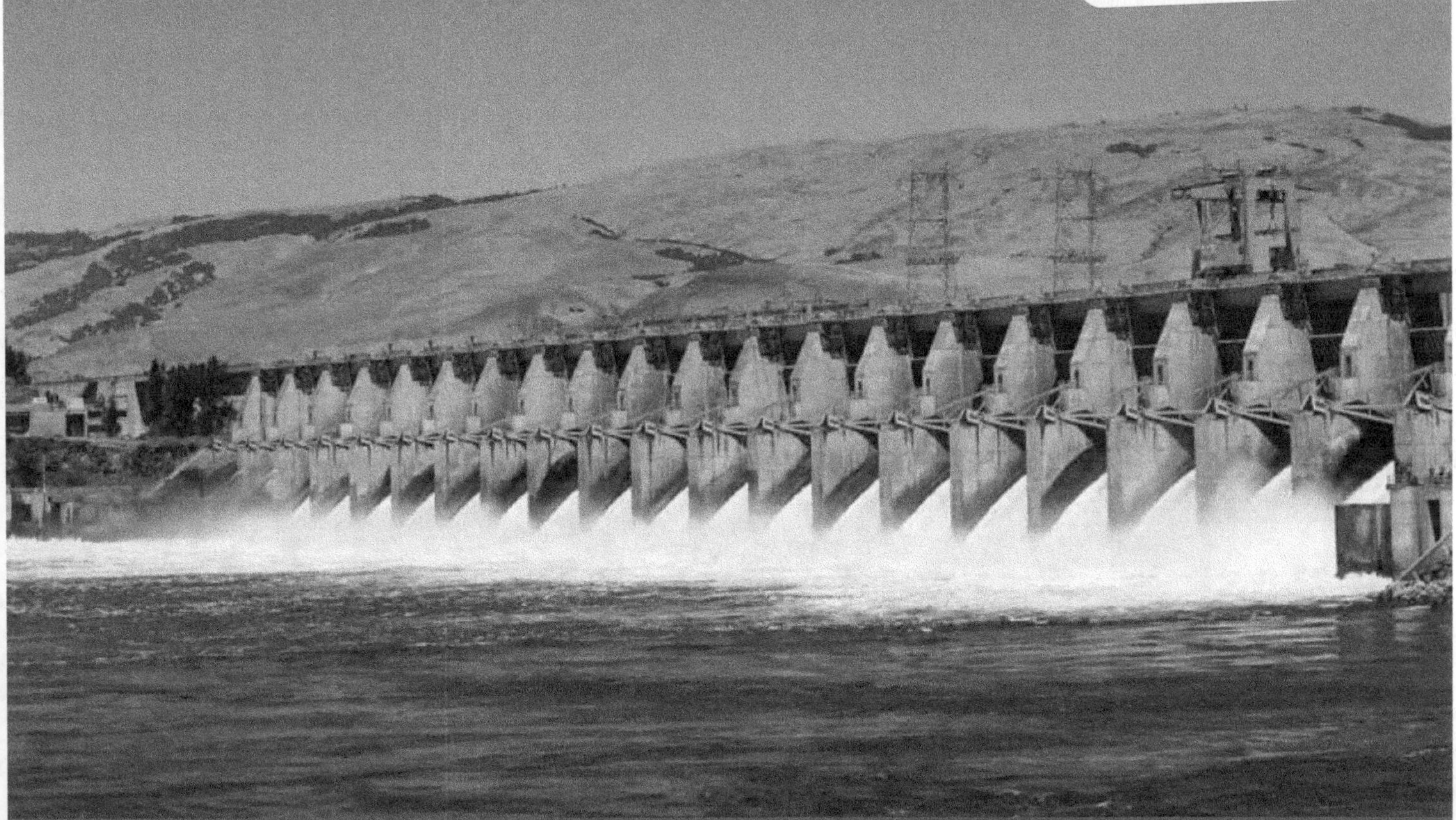

Dams
Sector-Specific Plan

An Annex to the National Infrastructure Protection Plan

2010

Homeland
Security

Preface

The National Infrastructure Protection Plan (NIPP) provides the unifying structure for the integration of critical infrastructure and key resources (CIKR) protection and resilience efforts as part of a coordinated national program. The NIPP provides the overarching framework for integrating protective programs and activities underway in the various sectors, as well as new and developing CIKR protection efforts. Sector-Specific Plans detail the application of the overall risk management framework to each of the 18 specific sectors.

The Dams Sector-Specific Plan (DSSP) was developed to complement the NIPP in achieving a safer, more secure, and more resilient Dams Sector by reducing vulnerabilities, deterring threats, and minimizing the consequences of terrorist attacks, natural disasters, and other incidents. Each year, the Dams Sector CIKR Protection Annual Report provides detailed updates on the efforts conducted by sector partners to identify, prioritize, and coordinate the protection of the sector's critical infrastructure. The Sector Annual Report describes the current priorities of the sector as well as the progress made during the past year in following the plans and strategies set out in the DSSP.

This 2010 release of the DSSP updates the original plan issued in May 2007. As with the original plan, this document was developed through active collaboration and coordination with Dams Sector partners. This plan, and the public-private partnership that it represents, supports the Nation's all-hazards approach to homeland security preparedness and domestic incident management. The 2010 release of the DSSP reflects the maturation of the Dams Sector partnership and its progress. Examples of Dams Sector accomplishments include the following:

- Developed, piloted, and successfully implemented the Consequence-Based Top Screen (CTS) methodology and supporting Web-based system to facilitate systematic screening and consistent prioritization of high-consequence assets across the sector.

- Developed multiple handbooks, guides, and Web-based training courses that emphasize risk-based protection and contingency planning to promote resilience.

- Developed simplified blast damage estimation models for dams, navigation locks, and levees and fostered interagency collaboration on studies to better understand the vulnerabilities of sector assets.

- Conducted several Dams Sector Exercise Series (DSES) efforts to identify, analyze, assess, and enhance regional preparedness and disaster resilience, using multi-jurisdictional discussion-based activities involving a wide array of public and private stakeholders.

- Implemented a strong framework for collaboration with stakeholders at the local, State, and regional level, and established the National Dam Security Forum as an effective outreach mechanism.

These achievements, which represent the effective collaboration of the Dams Sector Coordinating Council, Government Coordinating Council, and the Dams Sector-Specific Agency, clearly demonstrate the sector's progress in working toward a rational approach in the development, prioritization, and implementation of effective protective programs and resilience strategies.

In the same shared purpose that guided these actions and their support for the framework, concepts, and processes outlined in the NIPP, Dams Sector partners look forward to continuing their efforts to enhance the protection and resilience of our Nation's critical infrastructure and key resources.

Todd M. Keil

Assistant Secretary for
Infrastructure Protection
U.S. Department of Homeland Security

W. Craig Conklin

Director
SSA Executive Management Office
U.S. Department of Homeland Security
Chair, Dams GCC

Hal Dalson

Chair
Dams Sector
Coordinating Council

Table of Contents

List of Figures

List of Tables

Executive Summary

The Dams Sector-Specific Plan (DSSP) was developed to complement the National Infrastructure Protection Plan (NIPP) in achieving a safer, more secure, and more resilient Dams Sector by lessening vulnerabilities, deterring threats, and minimizing the consequences of terrorist attacks, natural disasters, and other incidents. This document updates the original Sector-Specific Plan issued in May 2007. As with the original plan, this document was developed through active collaboration and coordination with Dams Sector partners. This plan, and the public and private sector partnership that it represents, support the Nation's all-hazards approach to homeland security preparedness and domestic incident management. The DSSP portrays the collaborative partnership among all levels of government and the private sector that fosters the cooperation necessary to improve the protection and resilience of the Dams Sector. This plan describes the sector-wide processes required to identify and prioritize assets, assess risk in the sector, implement protective programs and resilience strategies, and measure their effectiveness.

Within the context of this document, protective programs and resilience strategies cover a wide range of on-site and off-site efforts, such as implementing active or passive countermeasures and improving security protocols; hardening or retrofitting facilities to improve their performance under extreme loadings, such as blast, earthquake, and so forth; and implementing cybersecurity measures. These efforts also include building redundancy and implementing backup systems to minimize disruptions or alleviate undesirable consequences, and incorporating hazard resistance into facility design.

Additional activities involve promoting robust training and exercises at multiple levels to mitigate potential consequences, enhancing business continuity planning, and designing and planning multi-scenario restoration and recovery actions. This requires establishing effective partnerships with emergency responders and implementing effective incident management protocols and risk communications strategies that take into consideration all required stakeholders. Employing a comprehensive systems approach to make sure that all relevant interdependent systems are appropriately taken into account, and developing life-cycle systems management approaches to ensure effective operation and sustainability under dynamic conditions that are likely to change along the facility life span are key elements of protective programs and resilience strategies.

This document represents the collaborative efforts of members from the private sector, numerous government agencies, and professional organizations, all dedicated to the protection and resilience of the infrastructure within the Dams Sector.

1. Sector Profile and Goals

The Dams Sector comprises dam projects, hydropower plants, navigation locks, levees, dikes, hurricane barriers, mine tailings and other industrial waste impoundments, and other similar water retention and water control facilities. Dam projects are complex facilities that may include multiple water impoundment or control structures, reservoirs, spillways, outlet works, powerhouses, and canals or aqueducts. In some cases, navigation locks are also part of the project. Levees (and flood risk reduction systems in general) may feature multiple components that include embankment sections, as well as floodwall sections, pumps and pumping stations, interior drainage works, flood damage reduction channels, and other important elements. For the purposes of the DSSP, the term "sector assets" is used to denote the facilities and systems included as part of the Dams Sector. The term "dams" is used to denote dam projects since it is the more commonly used term, and the term "levees" is used to denote levee projects or flood risk reduction systems. It is important to note that these terms encompass physical, cyber, and human elements.

The Dams Sector is a vital and beneficial part of the Nation's infrastructure and continuously provides a wide range of economic, environmental, and social benefits, including hydroelectric power, river navigation, water supply, wildlife habitat, waste management, flood control, and recreation. The potential risks in the event of asset failures, regardless of causation, within the Dams Sector are considerable and could result in significant destruction, including loss of life, massive property damage, and severe long-term consequences.

Most of the dams in the United States are privately owned. As a result of their importance to the Nation, it is reasonable that there would be a Federal role in coordinating Federal, State, and local efforts to provide dam safety and security to citizens. The Dams Sector Government Coordinating Council and the Dams Sector Coordinating Council enhance the relationships with all entities in the Dams Sector and facilitate the flow of information and accountability. The numerous Federal and State departments and agencies that serve as owners, operators, and regulators are discussed in chapter 1.

The DSSP presents the goals established by the Dams Sector to facilitate the incorporation of protective measures and resilience strategies to improve awareness, prevention, protection, response, and recovery. The eight Dams Sector goals are driven by a desire to reduce the risks to critical assets within the Dams Sector, and to ensure the continued economic use and enjoyment of this nationally critical infrastructure. The eight goals of the Dams Sector are as follows:

1. Build Dams Sector partnerships and improve communication among all critical infrastructure and key resources (CIKR) partners;
2. Identify Dams Sector composition, consequences, and critical assets;
3. Improve the Dams Sector's understanding of viable threats;
4. Identify Dams Sector vulnerabilities;
5. Identify the risks to Dams Sector critical assets;
6. Develop guidance on how the Dams Sector will manage risks;
7. Enhance the security and resilience of the Dams Sector through research and development (R&D) efforts; and
8. Identify and address interdependencies.

2. Identify Assets, Systems, and Networks

The identification of assets, systems, and networks and their interdependencies is necessary to help manage steady-state CIKR protection and resilience approaches, as well as to support the corresponding response efforts during an incident or emergency. The National Inventory of Dams (NID) is currently the primary method for identifying and maintaining general data on dams. The data contained in the NID can also be used to populate the Infrastructure Data Warehouse, a national infrastructure inventory under development by the U.S. Department of Homeland Security (DHS).

The Dams Sector Consequence-Based Top-Screen methodology also provides a vehicle for consolidation of general facility information, as well as consequence parameters for those facilities that are potentially associated with significant impacts in case of failure, damage, or disruption. Additional interagency coordination efforts involving multi-jurisdictional programs, such as the proposed expansion of the National Levee Database, will be required to complete the identification of the sector's assets, systems, and networks.

3. Assess Risks

From the security perspective, risk is defined as a function of three parameters: (1) threat, the likelihood of an attack being attempted against a target; (2) vulnerability, the susceptibility of a target to being compromised by an attack; and (3) consequence, the set of undesirable impacts of the attack, if successful. Rigorous risk models consider the threat and vulnerability parameters as probabilities; threat is defined as the probability of a given type of attack and vulnerability is defined as the probability that a given type of attack against the target will be successful. This is consistent with the definition of risk corresponding to natural hazards. In this case, risk is defined as a function of the probability that an event (such as an earthquake or flood) may occur; the probability that the facility may not perform to the required performance level (e.g., structural failure could be an example of unacceptable performance); and the corresponding consequences. Many agencies and companies that own or regulate dams in the United States have an extensive background in developing and applying methodologies for assessing risks and prioritizing their asset inventories. There are multiple risk assessment methodologies utilized across the Dams Sector that are well suited for owner use but are based on different assumptions and approaches, and generally do not follow a common terminology. This presents technical and logistical obstacles for sector-wide risk assessment efforts as it often results in unique solutions that cannot be easily compared. As a result, these methodologies, while extremely useful in their own right at the owner level for specific analyses, cannot meet the requirements and expectations at the national and sector levels.

A sector-wide risk assessment approach must satisfy the need for a practical methodology suitable for comprehensive sector-wide use and yield risk results that can be objectively compared across the sector. The desired sector-wide risk assessment model will make use of data from existing risk analyses, thus leveraging the efforts already made by owners and operators through facility-specific assessments, with the goal of conducting a sector-wide prioritization without having to collect or develop significant amounts of new data. This sector-wide risk assessment model will strive for the lowest achievable complexity and logistical burden while taking maximum advantage of existing assessments. The model needs to be simple, transparent, and easy to use, but also mathematically defensible and scalable to provide for more rigorous analyses, if needed.

The sector has well-established programs to assess, mitigate, and respond to the potential damages caused by catastrophic failures induced by natural hazards. The experience and body of knowledge developed by the dam and levee safety communities in the identification of structural and operational deficiencies with respect to the extreme demands imposed by natural hazards, and the quantification of potential failure consequences, are applicable to the risk assessment problem from the critical infrastructure protection perspective.

4. Prioritize Infrastructure

Consistent prioritization is essential to focus planning, foster coordination, and support effective resource allocation and incident management decisions supporting CIKR protection. To meet the overarching goal of prioritizing assets in a manner that is consistent across different CIKR sectors, the Dams Sector-Specific Agency (SSA) will seek the collaboration of all sector partners and other relevant stakeholders to design a risk management framework that facilitates such a sector-wide prioritization process. This prioritization process will ultimately assist in identifying the concerns, problems, and gaps that require the most urgent attention from a sector-wide perspective.

The prioritization process involves two different levels. The first level focuses on identifying and characterizing critical assets and systems, since it is assumed that they constitute the main drivers for the sector risk profile. The second level focuses on determining the sector-wide programs and strategies that would be most effective in response to the corresponding risk profile. The Dams SSA will work with all sector partners and request their input to update, refine, or develop, as necessary, sector and subsector screening methodologies that can be useful in identifying and categorizing critical assets and systems. This voluntary process of sector-wide collaboration will also be extended to the development of additional asset characterization methodologies that are required to more effectively define the vulnerability and attractiveness of those critical assets. The goal of these efforts is to facilitate the effective identification of those critical assets associated with the most severe consequences from a sector-wide perspective, and support a clear and consistent definition of their corresponding consequence and vulnerability variables affecting risk. This will facilitate the development of the comprehensive risk profile for the sector and support decisionmakers in the prioritization of protective programs and resilience strategies.

5. Develop and Implement Protective Programs and Resilience Strategies

From a comprehensive all-hazards perspective, protective programs and resilience strategies involve measures designed to prevent, detect, deter, and mitigate the threat; reduce vulnerability to an attack or other disaster; minimize consequences; and enable timely, efficient response and restoration in a post-event situation, whether a terrorist attack, natural disaster, or other incident. Protective programs in the Dams Sector will vary as a result of diverse and distinct assets, operational processes, business environments, and risk management approaches, as well as diversity in the missions and objectives of asset owners, operators, and regulators. Protective programs and resilience strategies guide owners and operators in implementing effective actions and include measures that address physical assets, cyber elements, and human resources. Development and implementation of protective programs and resilience strategies at the facility level involve determining appropriate threat or hazard scenarios, assessing the acceptable level of performance, identifying constraints, and designing and implementing the corresponding measures.

6. Measure Effectiveness

Measuring program effectiveness requires well-designed and efficiently gathered progress indicators that establish accountability, document actual performance, facilitate diagnoses, promote effective management, and provide feedback—all of which contribute to continued improvement in protective programs and resilience strategies. The goals and objectives of these programs and strategies dictate the data gathered and frame the forms in which data are gathered, from whom, and how they are reported. The use of outcome metrics, output data, and descriptive data allows CIKR partners to better coordinate their efforts and adjust the sector-wide protection approach to account for progress achieved and for changes in the sector's overall risk profile.

7. Critical Infrastructure and Key Resources Protection Research and Development

Research and development is one of the key tools used by the sector to improve knowledge pertaining to threats (manmade actions or natural hazards), vulnerabilities, consequences, and the subsequent risks associated with sector assets when subject to attacks or disasters. Dams Sector councils have highlighted the role of effective R&D initiatives in reducing risk within the sector and have identified enhancing the security and resilience of the Dams Sector through R&D efforts as a sector goal. The SSA and Dams Sector R&D Workgroup, comprised of both public and private council members, lead the activities to characterize sector research and technology needs, maintain awareness of the state-of-the-art technology and research related to those needs, and delineate the gaps between what is needed and what is available or known in order to develop an R&D plan. Sector R&D gaps and needs are selected and prioritized based on the risks to sector assets that have not yet been adequately addressed but have the potential to be resolved to the point that the risk can be disproven as a valid threat or managed or mitigated through physical or operational interventions that are cost-effective and operationally acceptable.

8. Manage and Coordinate Sector-Specific Agency Responsibilities

The SSA for the Dams Sector is the DHS Office of Infrastructure Protection, which executes its SSA responsibilities through the Sector-Specific Agency Executive Management Office. The SSA responsibilities are described in detail in the NIPP, and include identifying, prioritizing, and coordinating sector-wide CIKR protection and resilience activities; coordinating, facilitating, and supporting comprehensive risk assessment and risk management programs for high-risk assets and systems; identifying protection and resilience priorities; incorporating protection activities as a key component of the all-hazards approach to domestic incident management within the sector; facilitating the sharing of real-time incident notification, as well as CIKR protection recommended practices and guidelines; and promoting CIKR protection education, training, and awareness across the sector.

The Dams SSA will capitalize on the cooperation and coordination that already exists among sector partners to execute the assigned responsibilities and ensure that the sector meets its goals and objectives.

Introduction

The U.S. Department of Homeland Security (DHS) was established officially as an executive department of the United States with the enactment of the Homeland Security Act of 2002. The act assigns DHS the responsibility for developing a comprehensive national plan for securing the Nation's critical infrastructure[1] and key resources (CIKR), and recommending the "measures necessary to protect the key resources and critical infrastructure of the United States in coordination with other agencies of the Federal Government and in cooperation with State and local government agencies and authorities, the private sector, and other entities."

Protecting the CIKR of the United States is essential to the Nation's security, public health and safety, economic vitality, and way of life. Attacks on CIKR could lead to significant disruption of the functioning of government and business alike, and produce cascading effects far beyond the targeted sector and physical location of the incident. Direct terrorist attacks and natural, manmade, or technological hazards could produce catastrophic losses in terms of human casualties, destruction of property, and economic effects, as well as profound damage to public morale and confidence. Attacks using components of the Nation's CIKR as weapons of mass destruction could have even more devastating physical and psychological consequences.

The national approach for CIKR protection is provided through the unifying framework established in Homeland Security Presidential Directive 7 (HSPD-7). This directive establishes the U.S. policy for "enhancing protection of the Nation's CIKR" and mandates a national plan to actuate that policy. In HSPD-7, the President designates the Secretary of Homeland Security as the "principal Federal official to lead CIKR protection efforts among Federal departments and agencies, State and local governments, and the private sector." Eighteen CIKR sectors were established, each recognized as possessing unique characteristics and operating methods. The responsibility for CIKR sectors is designated to Sector-Specific Agencies (SSAs).

A comprehensive and well-coordinated protective strategy for all CIKR sectors is an essential component of the homeland security mission to make America safer, more secure, and more resilient to terrorist attacks and other hazards, natural or manmade. The National Infrastructure Protection Plan (NIPP) fulfills this important requirement by providing a coordinated approach to CIKR protection in which the plans and policies that owners and operators implement to prepare for, mitigate, respond to, and recover from a variety of natural and manmade incidents are augmented, as needed, by sector-level protective programs and resilience strategies that take advantage of sector and cross-sector collaboration. Many of the benefits of enhanced CIKR protection are most sustainable when these programs and strategies are designed to address all hazards.

Consistent with the all-hazards approach, infrastructure safety and infrastructure security are the goals of risk-informed protective programs that support life safety, economic stability, and general welfare. In the NIPP context, protection includes actions to mitigate the overall risk to CIKR assets, systems, networks, functions, or their interconnecting links, and actions to deter the

---

[1] See the Glossary of Terms for definitions of the terms used in this document.

threat, mitigate vulnerabilities, or minimize the consequences associated with a terrorist attack or other incident. Protection can include a wide range of activities, such as improving security protocols, hardening facilities, building resilience and redundancy, incorporating hazard resistance into facility design, initiating active or passive countermeasures, installing security systems, leveraging "self-healing" technologies, promoting workforce surety programs, implementing cybersecurity measures, training and exercises, business continuity planning, and restoration and recovery activities. The NIPP provides the framework for the cooperation that is needed to develop, implement, and maintain a coordinated national effort that brings together government at all levels, the private sector, regional coalitions, international organizations, and nongovernmental organizations.

A fundamental objective of the NIPP is to identify and protect infrastructure that is deemed *most critical*. The NIPP risk management framework, depicted in Figure I-1, supports prioritization of protection and resilience initiatives and investments across sectors to ensure that government and private sector resources are applied where they offer the most benefit. Within this risk-informed construct, consequences (direct impacts and those caused by sector interdependencies) are initial measures of infrastructure criticality which must then be assessed in the context of infrastructure vulnerabilities and potential threats. The resulting protective programs maximize risk reduction across the spectrum of relevant hazards.

Along with its complementary Sector-Specific Plans (SSPs), the NIPP provides a consistent, unifying structure for integrating both existing and future CIKR protection efforts within and across all sectors. The purpose of the SSPs is to detail the application of the NIPP risk management framework to each of the 18 CIKR sectors.

Figure I-1: NIPP Risk Management Framework

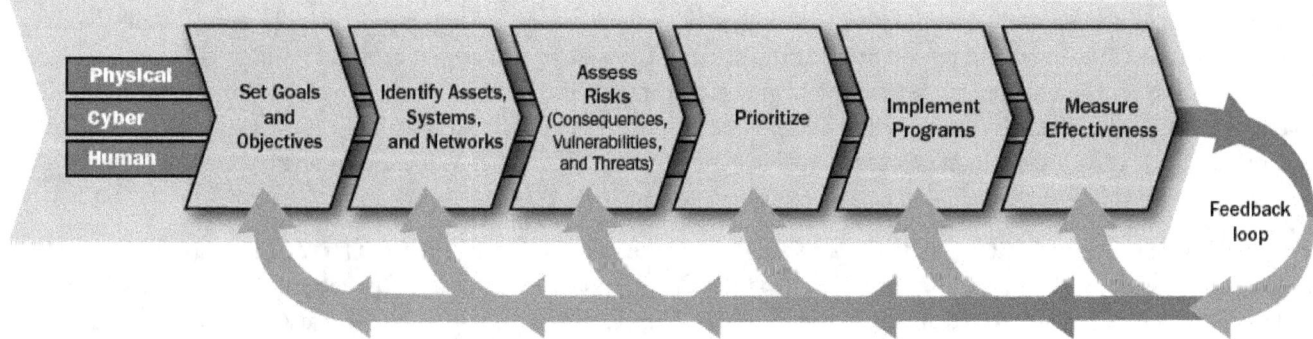

Continuous improvement to enhance protection of CIKR

This document is the Dams Sector-Specific Plan (DSSP). It aligns with the NIPP risk management framework and supports the planning assumptions outlined in the NIPP, as well as the sector-specific planning assumptions relevant to the protection and resilience of the Dams Sector.

This DSSP updates the original plan issued in May 2007. As with the original plan, this 2010 DSSP was developed by the designated SSA within the DHS Office of Infrastructure Protection (IP) in active coordination with sector partners.

This update describes several indicators of the continued collaboration among the Dams Sector Coordinating Council (SCC), the Levee Sub-Sector Coordinating Council (LSCC), the Dams Sector Government Coordinating Council (GCC), the Levee Sub-Sector Government Coordinating Council (LGCC), the SSA, and other partners to enhance CIKR protection and resilience in an all-hazards context such as the following:

• Formation of the LSCC and the LGCC to establish dedicated forums to address levee protection and resilience issues;

• Expansion of the GCC to strengthen cross-sector connections where dependencies and interdependencies exist;

- Creation of the State Dam Security Panel to enhance collaboration with the State dam safety offices that regulate more than 70,000 of the dams listed in the National Inventory of Dams (NID);

- Development of a cybersecurity roadmap outlining an effective framework to secure control systems within the sector;

- Production and dissemination of reference documents containing guidelines and recommendations on security awareness, protective measures, and crisis management;

- Development and implementation of the Consequence-Based Top-Screen methodology and corresponding Web-based tool to identify high-consequence assets;

- Implementation of information-sharing standard operating procedures to enhance sector-wide communication;

- Development and coordination of multi-jurisdictional exercises involving government and privately owned sector assets to enhance regional disaster resilience;

- Development of Web-based training modules that focus on the security awareness, protective measures, and crisis management issues relevant to the Dams Sector; and

- Coordination of an active research and development (R&D) agenda to address sector-determined risks.

The Dams Sector comprises dam projects, hydropower generation facilities, navigation locks, levees, dikes, hurricane barriers, mine tailings and other industrial waste impoundments, and other similar water retention and water control facilities. Dam projects are complex facilities that may include multiple water impoundment or control structures, reservoirs, spillways, outlet works, powerhouses, and canals or aqueducts. In some cases, navigation locks are also part of the dam project.

For the purposes of the DSSP and because of the particular and varied characteristics of the sector, a clear *asset-centric* approach will be used. The term "sector assets" will be used in general to denote the facilities and systems included as part of the Dams Sector. The term "dams" will be used to denote dam projects (encompassing their multiple components and their physical, cyber, and human elements) because that is the more commonly used term. Similarly, the term "levee" is meant to denote levee projects or flood risk reduction systems that may include embankment sections, floodwall sections, pumps and pumping stations, interior drainage works, closure structures, penetrations, and transitions.

The remainder of this DSSP is structured around each of the steps outlined in the NIPP risk management framework, which includes the following activities:

- **Set Goals and Objectives:** Define specific outcomes, conditions, end points, or performance targets that collectively define the risk management posture that CIKR partners seek to attain.

- **Identify Infrastructure:** Develop an inventory of critical assets and systems and their functions, including infrastructure located outside the United States, and collect information pertinent to risk management.

- **Assess Risks:** Determine risk by combining the potential direct and indirect consequences of a terrorist attack or other hazard (including the dependencies and interdependencies associated with each identified asset or system), known vulnerabilities to various potential attack vectors, and general or specific threat information.

- **Prioritize:** Aggregate and analyze assessment results to determine infrastructure criticality, and develop a risk-informed framework to establish sector-wide priorities and provide the basis for improved sector-wide protective programs and resilience strategies and effective allocation of resources.

- **Implement Programs:** Select appropriate risk management actions or programs to reduce the risk identified and secure the resources needed to address priorities.

- **Measure Effectiveness:** Use metrics and other approaches, as appropriate, to examine and evaluate the effectiveness of efforts to achieve sector goals and priorities.

1. Dams Sector Profile and Goals

A distinct characteristic of the Dams Sector is that each owner or operator has unique assets, operational processes, business environments, and risk management approaches that vary across all business lines because of the considerable diversity of owners, operators, and regulators in this sector. This chapter provides a short historical perspective and a characterization of the Dams Sector; identifies Dams Sector partners and their roles and responsibilities; and describes the sector's goals, objectives, and desired long-term security and resilience posture.

1.1 Dams Sector Profile

Dams Sector assets include dam projects, hydropower generation facilities, navigation locks, levees, dikes, hurricane barriers, mine tailings and other industrial waste impoundments, and other similar water retention and water control facilities. The majority of the statistics provided in the following sections are based on data from the NID, which contains information on dams only. Additional information about this database is provided in chapter 2. Although basic information on many sector assets is readily available through the NID, quantifying and characterizing other assets, such as levees, hurricane barriers, and mine tailings and other industrial waste impoundments, remain important challenges for the sector. Complete identification of the sector's landscape will require significant interagency collaboration at the Federal, State, and local levels to leverage available resources and maximize collaboration with other programs.

1.1.1 Benefits and Risks

The rapid growth of the American economy and population in the 20th century caused a corresponding increase in the demand for water infrastructure projects. Legislation such as the Reclamation Act of 1902; the Tennessee Valley Authority (TVA) Act of 1933; and the Flood Control Acts of 1928, 1936, and 1938 resulted in construction of a large number of dams and levees. Dam building in the United States peaked during the 30 years following World War II, when more than half of the Nation's current total of 82,642 NID-listed dams was built.[2]

Prior to the 1930s, levees were constructed haphazardly, without the benefit of good engineering practices, and generally to protect agricultural areas. Disastrous floods on the Mississippi and Ohio rivers spurred the U.S. Congress to pass the Flood Control Acts of 1928 and 1936, which established a direct Federal interest in the design and construction of levees.[3] Although the total number is currently unknown, a recent estimate is that there may be as many as 100,000 miles of levees in the

---

[2] Based on the most current NID update, 2009.

[3] Recommendations for a National Levee Safety Program (draft), January 2009.

Nation.[4] The aftermath of hurricanes Katrina and Rita turned the attention of Congress once more to levees and it passed the National Levee Safety Act of 2007.

Dams Sector assets are vital components of the Nation's infrastructure and continuously provide a wide range of economic, environmental, and social benefits, including hydroelectric power, river navigation, water supply, wildlife habitat, waste management, flood risk reduction, and recreation, just to name a few. Some examples of the benefits derived from sector assets are discussed below:

- **Water Storage and Irrigation:** Dams create reservoirs throughout the United States that supply water for a multitude of industrial, municipal, agricultural, and recreational uses. Ten percent of American cropland is irrigated by using water stored behind dams and thousands of jobs are tied to producing crops grown with irrigation water.

- **Electricity Generation:** The United States is one of the largest producers of hydropower in the world, second only to Canada. Dams in the United States produce more than 270,000 gigawatt-hours, contributing 7 percent of the Nation's electricity and representing 70 percent of the Nation's renewable energy generation.

- **"Black Start" Capabilities:** There are 4,316 megawatts of "incremental" hydropower available at sites with existing hydroelectric facilities. Incremental hydropower is defined as capacity additions or improved efficiency at existing hydro projects. During the August 2003 blackout in the Northeast, hydropower projects in New York and several other States were able to quickly start generating electricity, leading the way to restoring power to millions of Americans.

- **Recreation:** Dams and other sector assets provide prime recreational facilities throughout the United States. In 2002, a total of 105.7 million recreation user-days and -nights were provided at hydropower projects licensed by the Federal Energy Regulatory Commission (FERC). In addition, about 400 million people annually visit a project of the U.S. Army Corps of Engineers (USACE), and about 90 million visit a project of the Bureau of Reclamation in a year.

- **Navigation:** Navigational projects constitute an essential component of the U.S. waterway system, which includes 236 lock chambers at 192 lock sites owned and/or operated by USACE. A principal value of the inland and intracoastal navigation system is the ability to efficiently convey large volumes of bulk commodities moving long distances. If the cargo transported on the inland waterways each year had to be moved by another mode, it would take an additional 6.3 million rail cars or 25.2 million trucks to carry the load. The ability to move more cargo per shipment makes barge transport both fuel-efficient and environmentally advantageous.

- **Flood Risk Reduction:** Many dams and levees function as flood control projects, thereby reducing the potential human health and economic impacts of flooding. Reservoirs and levees built by USACE reportedly prevented more than $19 billion in potential damages during the 1993 Midwest Flood. USACE levee systems currently provide a 6:1 return on flood damages prevented compared to initial costs and robust levee systems provide a 24:1 return on investments. Levees and hurricane barriers reduce flood damage to rural communities, as well as major metropolitan areas.

- **Sediment Control:** Some dams enhance environmental protection by controlling detrimental sedimentation.

- **Impoundment of Mine Tailings and Industrial Waste Materials:** More than 1,500 mine tailings and industrial waste impoundments controlled by dams in the Nation facilitate mining and processing of coal and other vital minerals and manufacturing while protecting the environment.

The benefits of these sector assets, however, are countered by the magnitude of the consequences that could be associated with their potential failure, damage, or disruption. The 42-foot-high embankment Laurel Run Dam near Johnstown, Pennsylvania, was overtopped and breached in 1977 after exceptionally heavy rain and serves as a modern reminder of the potential conse-

---

[4] Recommendations for a National Levee Safety Program (draft), January 2009.

quences of asset failure. Forty people died as a result of the failure and damages were estimated at $5.3 million.[5] The potential for catastrophic consequences associated with extreme flooding and severe storm surges was evidenced in the aftermath of hurricanes Katrina and Rita in 2005, which resulted in the deaths of more than 1,800 people and economic damages estimated at more than $200 billion.[6] More recently, the 2008 Midwest flooding event affected significant urban and agricultural areas across a number of States, including Illinois, Indiana, Iowa, Michigan, Minnesota, Missouri, and Wisconsin, causing considerable property damage. Natural hazards such as severe regional floods can occur almost anywhere in the Nation and they clearly represent a significant factor in the complex risk picture of the Dams Sector. Extreme hydrological events can overwhelm the flood storage capacity of reservoirs and levee systems and raise the possibility of breaching or overtopping.

In another example, the near failure of the 142-foot-high Lower San Fernando Dam during a magnitude 6.7 earthquake forced the evacuation of more than 80,000 people in the San Fernando Valley of southern California in 1971.[7] This dam, which suffered severe seismic-induced damage, had been constructed with methods that did not provide adequate resistance to earthquake shaking. Analytical methods and seismic assessment procedures have greatly improved in recent years; however, it is still not possible to reliably predict the behavior of dams during strong ground shaking. A number of high-consequence assets are located in active seismic areas and their potential exposure to severe earthquakes constitutes a significant risk.

Droughts have the potential to affect hydropower production with the cascading impact of higher electricity costs as companies and power marketers must purchase power on the open market to meet customer needs. The 2007 drought affecting the Apalachicola-Chattahoochee-Flint river basin in the Southeast raised concerns about the capability of the basin's hydroelectric facilities to continue functioning.[8] An assessment of the projected effects of drought on electric power generation in the Nation's Western Electricity Coordinating Council system revealed that hydroelectric production could drop by almost 30 percent in a severe drought year; in typical years, approximately 28 percent of the system's electric power capacity is supplied by hydropower, in wet hydrologic years it can rise to 40 percent. Additionally, electricity generated from coal would also drop as coal-fired plants would not have access to cooling water. Although natural gas plants could supply the electricity not supplied by hydropower or coal, the cost of electricity would increase.[9]

These historical references provide a framework to highlight the importance of an all-hazards approach to risk management for the Dams Sector. The sector contains a number of high-consequence assets whose failure could cause sudden downstream flooding, resulting in a significant number of casualties and catastrophic economic impact. The consequences of a deliberate attack or serious natural disaster on any of these critical assets could be wide-ranging and depend on a number of variables, including the type of facility, the failure or disruption mode, critical functions (e.g., water supply, hydroelectric power generation, navigation, etc.), system redundancies, downstream population density, regional infrastructure, and seasonal conditions.

Given the many different assets within the Dams Sector, a number of failure modes and mission disruption scenarios could be theoretically within reach of determined aggressors with the necessary capabilities. This potential is a matter of special concern in the case of high-consequence facilities and constitutes an important element in the sector risk profile. The combined effects of growing downstream development, insufficient maintenance funding, continuous aging, inadequate past design practices, and exposure to potential extreme events caused by natural hazards or deliberate aggressor actions drive a complex risk picture that could affect millions of people located in the path of a sudden dam or levee failure.

---

[5] http://www.damsafety.org/news/?p=94bdfdd0-633a-4fa2-bc39-0083c58d14ba, accessed September 1, 2009.

[6] Recommendations for a National Levee Safety Program (draft), January 2009.

[7] http://cee.engr.ucdavis.edu/faculty/boulanger/geo_photo_album/Earthquake%20hazards/LSF%20dam/LSF%20dam%20-%20Main.html, accessed September 1, 2009.

[8] Apalachicola-Chattahoochee-Flint (ACF) Drought: Federal Reservoir and Species Management, Congressional Research Service, RL34250, November 14, 2007.

[9] An Analysis of the Effects of Drought Conditions on Electric Power Generation in the Western United States, National Energy Technology Laboratory, DOE/NETL-2009/1365, April 2009.

The safety and security communities within the Dams Sector share the same interest of minimizing potential impacts resulting from failure or disruption. A coordinated approach to enhance the reliability, safety, security, and resilience of Dams Sector assets is required to address the entire spectrum of its risk profile through practical and cost-effective solutions.

1.1.2 Characterization of Dams Sector Assets

As previously described, sector assets encompass a broad spectrum of facilities. These facilities are found throughout the Nation.

1.1.2.1 Dams

Dams are facilities that include some or all of the following components to perform their intended purposes: a conventional dam or impounding structure (structural sections that hold back the water), a reservoir (a body of water impounded by the dam), spillways (structures that facilitate the discharge of normal and/or flood flows in a manner that protects the structural integrity of the project), outlet works (a combination of structures and equipment required for safe operation and control of water released from a reservoir), a powerhouse (a structure that houses turbines, generators, and associated control equipment for the production of hydroelectricity), penstocks (pipelines or conduits used to convey water under pressure to turbines or pump units), and canals/aqueducts (constructed channels, usually open, that convey water by gravity and also may be used for navigational purposes). Figure 1-1 depicts some of the multi-functional components that can be found at a project.

In general, canals convey water within an open channel from a source to a destination and can serve a variety of functions. Some canals, constructed as part of water supply or transportation projects, have an embankment section forming one of the sides of the water conveyance structure and acting as a water retention structure. Water can be conveyed for a variety of uses (e.g., domestic, municipal, industrial, or agricultural water supply) or as a means of transportation for boats, barges, or other watercraft. In some cases, dams also include navigation locks.

Dams may be classified according to the type of construction materials used, the methods of construction, the slope or cross-section, the way that the structure resists the forces of the water pressure behind it, the means used for controlling seepage, the purpose, and the hazard potential. Materials used for construction include earth, rock, tailings from mining or milling, concrete, masonry, steel, timber, miscellaneous materials such as plastic or rubber, or any combination of these materials. The two most common types of dams in use today are embankment dams and concrete dams.[10]

---

[10] Association of State Dam Safety Officials (ASDSO), Introduction to Dams, **http://www.damsafety.org**.

Figure 1-1: Multi-Functional Components of a Project

Embankment dams are the most common type of dam in use today. An embankment dam is termed an "earthfill" or "rock-fill" dam, depending on whether it is composed of compacted earth or mostly compacted or dumped rock. The ability of an embankment dam to resist the reservoir water pressure is primarily a result of the mass weight and the type and strength of the materials from which the dam is made.

Concrete dams may be categorized as gravity or arch dams. In concrete gravity dams, the most common form of concrete dam, the weight of the concrete and the friction force along the foundation are used to resist the reservoir water pressure. Gravity dams are constructed of vertical blocks of concrete with flexible seals in the joints between the blocks. A buttress dam is a specific type of gravity dam in which the large mass of concrete is reduced, and the forces are diverted to the dam foundation through vertical or sloping buttresses. Concrete arch dams are characterized by thinner cross-sections in which the reservoir water pressure is carried laterally into the abutments. The shape of the arch may resemble a segment of a circle or an ellipse, and the arch may be curved in the vertical plane as well. Such dams are usually constructed of a series of thin vertical blocks that are keyed together; barriers to stop water from flowing are provided between the blocks. Variations of arch dams include multi-arch dams in which more than one curved section is used and arch-gravity dams that combine some features of the two types of dams.

The NID currently lists 82,642 dams in the United States; more than 70,000 of them are State-regulated, 4,639 are regulated by Federal agencies, and the remainder is not regulated by any government agency. The ownership of dams in the United States makes them a unique part of the national infrastructure. Although most infrastructure facilities, such as roads, bridges, and sewer systems, are owned by public entities, the majority of dams (almost 65 percent) in the United States are owned by private entities. Figure 1-2 illustrates the ownership structure and primary purposes of dams in the United States.

Figure 1-2: Ownership and Primary Purpose of U.S. Dams

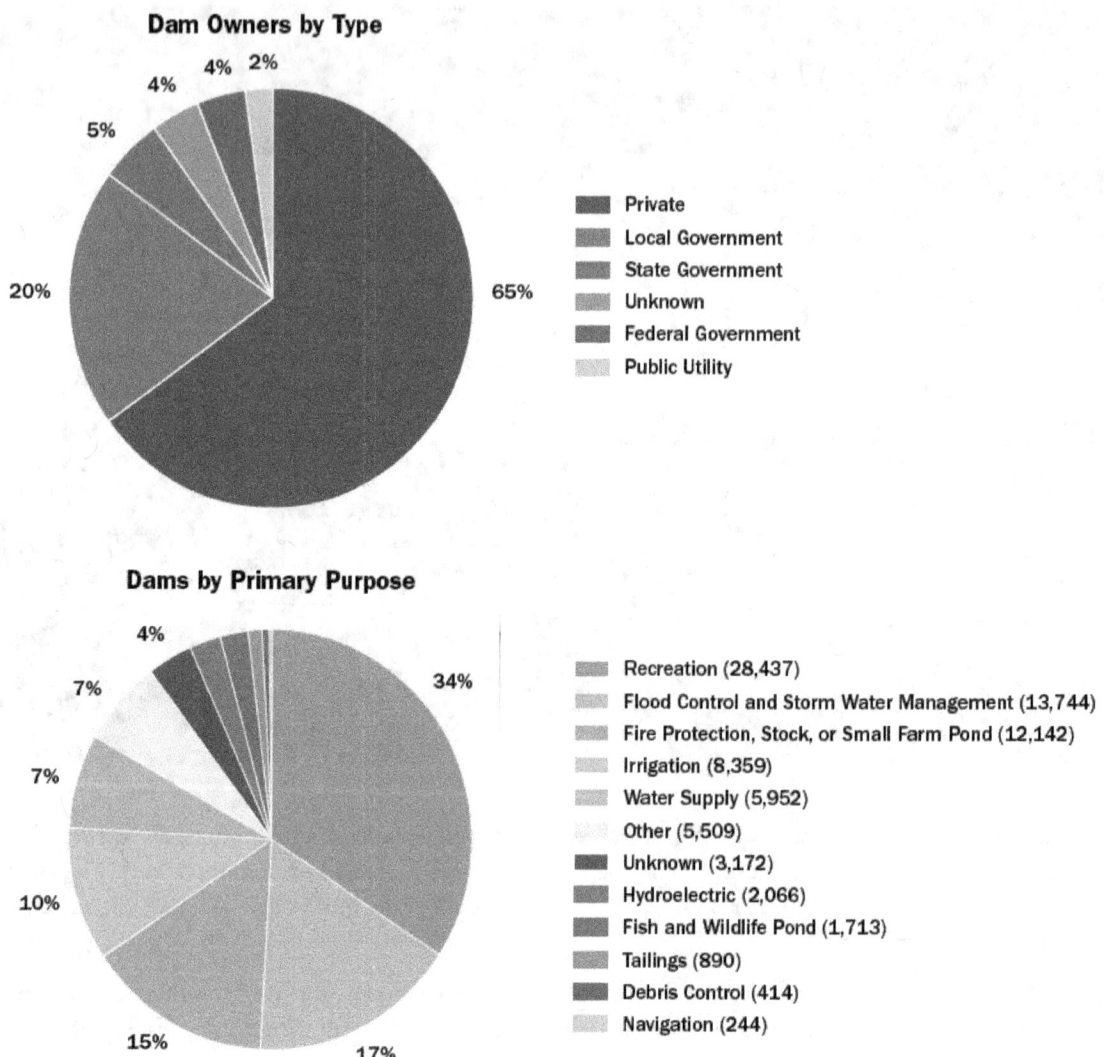

Dam Owners by Type

- Private — 65%
- Local Government — 20%
- State Government — 5%
- Unknown — 4%
- Federal Government — 4%
- Public Utility — 2%

Dams by Primary Purpose

- Recreation (28,437) — 34%
- Flood Control and Storm Water Management (13,744) — 17%
- Fire Protection, Stock, or Small Farm Pond (12,142) — 15%
- Irrigation (8,359) — 10%
- Water Supply (5,952) — 7%
- Other (5,509) — 7%
- Unknown (3,172) — 4%
- Hydroelectric (2,066)
- Fish and Wildlife Pond (1,713)
- Tailings (890)
- Debris Control (414)
- Navigation (244)

1.1.2.2 Navigation Locks

The term "navigation lock" is used to denote navigation projects that include the locks themselves (single or multiple chambers), as well as the associated dam (unless located in a canal), and a number of appurtenant structures such as approach walls, control rooms, and administration and maintenance buildings. The U.S. waterway system includes 236 lock chambers at 192 lock sites owned and/or operated by USACE. Many navigation projects may serve multiple purposes in addition to the primary navigation function. For example, 46 lock-associated dams currently produce hydropower.

These facilities make many inland waterways viable, year-round transportation corridors. Natural river beds are often long, uneven downhill slopes with shallow areas and deep pools. Water depths can vary with seasonal rainfall and snow melt; dry periods can significantly affect navigation. Locks on navigable rivers enable commercial and recreational river traffic to move safely from one pool level to the next. The lift of the locks—the difference between raising or lowering from one pool to the next—can range from just a few feet to 110 feet (e.g., John Day Lock and Dam on the Columbia River, Oregon and Washington).

Multiple locks may be part of one navigable river system. The Tennessee River system is managed through a series of dams and navigation locks owned by the United States and operated by TVA and USACE. The system's nine main and five auxiliary locks allow smooth movement on the river as it drops 513 feet in elevation from its beginning to the point at which it joins the Ohio River. The Mississippi River is made navigable through a total of 30 main and 4 auxiliary locks.

A principal value of the inland and intracoastal navigation system is the ability to efficiently convey large volumes of bulk commodities moving long distances. Towboats push barges lashed together to form a "tow." A 15-barge tow is common on larger rivers with locks, such as the Ohio, Upper Mississippi, Illinois, and Tennessee rivers. Such tows are an extremely efficient mode of transportation, moving about 22,500 tons of cargo as a single unit. A single 15-barge tow is the equivalent of about 225 rail cars or 870 tractor-trailer trucks. If the cargo transported on the inland waterways each year had to be moved by another mode, it would take an additional 6.3 million rail cars or 25.2 million trucks to carry the load. The ability to move more cargo per shipment makes barge transport both fuel-efficient and environmentally advantageous. On average, a gallon of fuel allows 1 ton of cargo to be shipped 155 miles by truck, 413 miles by railway, and 576 miles by barge. As a result, cargo transported by barge results in an average transportation savings of about $11 per ton over the cost of shipping by alternative modes. Environmental advantage can also be measured by comparing the greenhouse gas (GHG) emissions produced during fuel consumption. On average, the tons of GHG emissions produced per million ton-miles are 71.61 by truck, 26.88 by railway, and 19.27 by barge.

Coal is the largest commodity by volume moving on the inland waterways. The Nation's electric industry depends on inland waterways for more than 20 percent of the coal that it consumes to produce electricity. Petroleum is the next largest group, including crude oil, gasoline, diesel fuel, jet fuel, heavy fuel oils, and asphalt. Another large group includes grain and other farm products, most of which move by waterway to ports on the Lower Mississippi or Columbia Rivers for export overseas. Sixty percent of the country's farm exports travel through inland waterways. Other major commodities include aggregates, such as stone, sand, and gravel used in construction; chemicals, including fertilizers; metal ores, minerals, and products, such as steel; and many other manufactured products.

1.1.2.3 Levees

The term "levee" is used to denote manmade flood risk reduction systems (e.g., embankment sections, floodwalls, closure structures, pumps, interior drainage works, and flood damage reduction channels) with the primary purpose of furnishing some level of protection from seasonal high water (floods), storm surges, precipitation, and other weather events.

Most levees are therefore subject to water loading for periods of only a few days or weeks per year, but obviously must be built where they are most needed. Accordingly, levees are built near or along rivers and coastlines that may be environmentally or hydrologically sensitive areas, which may complicate their design, construction, maintenance, and access for routine maintenance and emergency response. Typically, a levee will parallel a watercourse rather than be perpendicular to it, as in the case of conventional dams. In addition, there is often a greater degree of freedom in where a dam will be placed.

Levees, as opposed to dams, are geospatially extended systems that can run for multiple miles; however, the levee system may consist of several segments under different governance units. This creates opportunities for multiple failure modes and points throughout the system. Proper levee maintenance is often overlooked because it appears to be fairly basic—repair erosion damage, protect against unwanted vegetation growth or animal burrowing, and so forth—so it may be given low priority or ignored completely.

Levees are intended to reduce flood damage and are built to specific levels of protection (e.g., 100-year flood event plus 2 feet of freeboard). The level of protection will vary from project to project. The default design standard for levees has been either the 100-year standard associated with the National Flood Insurance Program or the level of protection ensuing from applying a Federal, development-oriented policy that attempts to maximize the national economic development return to the Nation.

However, to minimize risk and maximize public safety, the Nation is beginning to design levees to afford levels of protection commensurate with the risk that they are protecting against.

Levees are owned by Federal, State, local, or tribal governments, or private entities, but the total number of levees is unknown. There are more than 2,000 Federal levee systems under USACE authorities, totaling more than 14,000 miles of infrastructure; another 8,000 miles of levee-like structures along canals are federally owned and an additional 78,000 miles of non-federally owned levees may exist.[11]

Levee ownership and maintenance profiles are summarized as follows:

- **Federally Built, Owned, Operated, and Maintained:** These levees are part of flood protection projects that were authorized by Congress and built, owned, operated, and maintained by USACE; the United States Section of the International Boundary and Water Commission (IBWC); and other Federal agencies.

- **Federally Built and Locally Owned, Operated, and Maintained:** These levee projects were constructed by USACE but were turned over to a local sponsor (e.g., State, county, city, town, special district, federally recognized Indian tribe or tribal organization, Alaska Native Corporation, or any political subpart of a State or group of States) to own, operate, and maintain.

- **Included in the Rehabilitation and Inspection Program:** These levees were not federally built but are incorporated into the USACE Rehabilitation and Inspection Program at the request of the local community. An initial eligibility inspection must be performed by USACE, and projects can only stay in the program if they are properly maintained and operated by the local community.

- **Non-Federally (e.g., State or Local Government or Private) Built, Owned, Operated, and Maintained:** These levees encompass a flood protection project that was not authorized by Congress or any other Federal agency authority.

Levee ownership and governance patterns can sometimes be politically, socially, and economically more complex than those for dams. Levee activities may be cost-shared among agencies at several levels of government, which can contribute to delays in repairs and response and mitigation actions. Actual ownership, especially for older levees, may be unclear and may require lengthy litigation before the necessary repairs can be undertaken. Unclear ownership of levees and the levee segments that contribute to a levee system complicates the coordination and communication required for levee safety and resilience.

1.1.2.4 Hurricane Barriers

Hurricane barriers restrict the inflow of storm surges from hurricanes and extratropical storms into bays, estuaries, rivers and streams, and/or onto the adjacent lowlands. These barriers normally consist of gates that are closed during storms from a fully open position or partially open position, depending on the degree of routine use that they also serve.

Hurricane barriers in the Northeast that protect against flooding in large bays are normally left fully open and are closed only during a storm. Barriers in southern Florida serve a routine water control purpose and are completely closed during a hurricane event.

Hurricane barriers are typically large steel structures. Each of the movable gates that span the Providence River in Providence, Rhode Island is 40 feet wide and weighs 53 tons. Hurricane barriers are usually composed of at least two gates—one on each bank of the channel—but more complex configurations may include multiple gates that can be independently raised or closed depending on the surge volume.

---

[11] Recommendations for a National Levee Safety Program (draft), January 15, 2009.

The mining industry, electric power generation, and manufacturing industries often use impoundment structures to store and dewater waste. In the coal industry, embankment structures used for the disposal of fine coal waste are referred to as slurry impoundments; in other extractive industries, the structures used for the disposal of fine mine waste are referred to as tailings ponds. In other industries, they may be referred to as surface or industrial waste impoundments. The primary goal of these impoundments is the storage of tailings or mine waste, which are transported suspended in water and settle out in the impoundment.

These impoundments typically have features similar to dams, including key trenches, internal drains, filters, spillways, and outlet works. Some industrial impoundments, particularly large diked structures in arid regions, are constructed without spillways or outlet works and are designed instead to store the design storm quantity above the maximum normal pool and draw the pool back down using floating-pump systems. Stormwater diversions may also be used to divert water around the pond to preserve its integrity during heavy rainfall.

Impoundments pose possible health and safety risks to the surrounding population and property if breached. The typical size of impoundments has grown over the years, with some measuring more than 20,000 acre-feet and hundreds of feet high. Unlike traditional dam structures, waste material may be released with any breach, causing environmental damage to downstream or down-valley ecosystems. In addition to aboveground risk of failure, impoundments at mine sites, such as those located above coal mines in the Appalachian region, may break through to underground active or inactive mines if not constructed with regard to the underlying workings. Past spills at mine sites, processing facilities, and coal ash locations illustrate the hazards inherent in these waste containment structures.

Impoundments can be subject to Federal and/or State regulations. For example, as authorized by the Federal Mine Safety and Health Act, the Mine Safety and Health Administration regulations require approved plans for dams at coal mines if the dam impounds water, sediment, or slurry to an elevation of 5 feet or more above the upstream toe with a storage volume of 20 acre-feet or more; impounds water, sediment, or slurry 20 feet or more above the upstream toe; or presents a hazard to miners as determined by the local district manager.

In general, the construction and operation of these impoundment sites may be regulated by various entities, with the States playing a key role in oversight. Depending on its type, an impoundment could be subject to regulation by the Mine Safety and Health Administration, the Office of Surface Mining Dam Safety Program within the U.S. Department of the Interior, the Office of Water and the Office of Solid Waste and Emergency Response within the U.S. Environmental Protection Agency (EPA), and/or State and local authorities.

1.1.3 Cyber Infrastructure

As with many CIKR sectors, cyber infrastructure plays a key role in the operation and maintenance of many of the Dams Sector's complex facilities. Computer technology, information systems and communications technology are not only used to support day-to-day functions and operations, but also to provide essential support to the entire spectrum of business processes and organizational requirements across the sector.

Control systems are used either onsite or remotely to control and/or monitor the operations of the various types of facilities within the sector. Traditionally, control systems have consisted of stand-alone systems, in many cases, isolated from external effects. Because of the convergence of technologies, capabilities, and lower costs, these once isolated systems are frequently replaced or upgraded to newer, integrated systems that may be linked across networks with common communication protocols and access points. This has the potential to expose these systems to the same types of security vulnerabilities that have focused the attention of the information technology (IT) community. The following sections address these issues in more detail.

1.1.3.1 Control Systems

A control system is a device or group of devices that manages, commands, directs, or regulates the behavior of other devices or groups of devices. The term "control system" is synonymous with industrial control system (ICS), which is used to generally denote an information system used to control a process, including industrial processes (e.g., manufacturing, refining, etc.) and infrastructure-related processes (e.g., water treatment, water distribution, power generation, etc.).

Industrial control systems include supervisory control and data acquisition (SCADA) systems, distributed control systems (DCS), and smaller control systems that use programmable logic controllers to control localized processes. The term "SCADA" usually refers to centralized systems that monitor and control entire sites or complexes of systems spread over large areas. The monitoring aspects of a SCADA system are normally conducted through sensors placed throughout the system to collect the needed data. Most control actions are performed automatically by remote terminal units or by programmable logic controllers.

In contrast, controller elements in distributed control systems are not central in location, but instead are distributed throughout the system with each component subsystem controlled by one or more controllers. The entire system of controllers is connected by networks for communication and monitoring. In addition, DCS elements may directly connect to physical equipment such as switches, pumps, and valves or may work through an intermediate system such as a SCADA system.

Until recently, control systems had little resemblance to traditional information systems in that they were isolated systems running proprietary software and control protocols. However, as these systems have been increasingly integrated more closely into mainstream organizational information systems to promote connectivity, efficiency, and remote access capability, they have started to resemble the more traditional information systems. Increasingly, ICS uses the same commercially available hardware and software components as those in the organization's traditional information systems. While the change in industrial control system architecture supports new information system capabilities, it also provides significantly less isolation from the outside world for these systems, introducing many of the same vulnerabilities that exist in current networked information systems.

1.1.3.2 Cyber Standards for Hydroelectric Facilities

In response to the power blackout in 2003 in the northeastern United States, the North American Electric Reliability Corporation (NERC) promoted the development of a new mandatory system of reliability standards and compliance that would be backstopped by FERC. These standards would focus on ensuring that all entities responsible for the reliability of the bulk electric systems in the United States identify and protect critical cyber assets that control or could impact the reliability of those systems.

In August 2003, an interim "urgent action" cybersecurity standard (designated UA 1200) was initially adopted by NERC and was later proposed as a permanent standard (designated NERC 1300) in August 2005. In May 2006, a revised and modified version of NERC 1300 was developed under NERC's American National Standards Institute accreditation process (which incorporated thousands of comments from experts and operations personnel) and was subsequently adopted by NERC as the Critical Infrastructure Protection (CIP) Reliability Standards, CIP-001-1 through CIP-009-1.

In January 2008, FERC issued Order 706, Mandatory Reliability Standards for Critical Infrastructure, which approved eight CIP Reliability Standards, CIP-002-1 through CIP-009-1 (CIP-001-1 was previously approved in November 2006). These eight CIP standards were subsequently revised by NERC and approved by FERC in September 2009 with an effective date of April 1, 2010. The standards were labeled CIP-002-2 through CIP-009-2 to reflect revision 2. These standards are mandatory and require bulk power system users, owners, and operators, including hydroelectric power plants, to identify and document cyber risks and vulnerabilities, establish controls to secure critical cyber assets from physical and cyber sabotage, report security incidents, establish plans for recovery in the event of an emergency, and certify their level of compliance. Entities to which the standards apply are subject to NERC audits and fines for noncompliance.

Descriptions of the CIP standards are provided below. As these standards may be subject to future revision, the suffix that denotes the revision status (e.g., -2) is not included in the list:

- CIP-001, **Sabotage Reporting:** Requires a responsible entity to define, process, and track disturbances or unusual occurrences suspected or determined to be caused by sabotage and report them to the appropriate governmental agencies and/or regulatory bodies.

- CIP-002, **Critical Cyber Asset Identification:** Requires a responsible entity to identify its critical assets and critical cyber assets using a risk-based assessment methodology.

- CIP-003, **Security Management Controls:** Requires a responsible entity to develop and implement security management controls to protect critical cyber assets identified pursuant to CIP-002.

- CIP-004, **Personnel and Training:** Requires personnel with access to critical cyber assets to have identity verifications and criminal background checks. It also requires employee training.

- CIP-005, **Electronic Security Perimeters:** Requires the identification and protection of an electronic security perimeter and access points. The electronic perimeter is to encompass the critical cyber assets identified pursuant to the methodology required by CIP-002.

- CIP-006, **Physical Security of Critical Cyber Assets:** Requires a responsible entity to create and maintain a physical security plan that ensures that all cyber assets within an electronic perimeter are kept in an identified physical security perimeter.

- CIP-007, **Systems Security Management:** Requires a responsible entity to define the methods, processes, and procedures for securing the systems identified as critical cyber assets, as well as the noncritical cyber assets within an electronic security perimeter.

- CIP-008, **Incident Reporting and Response Planning:** Requires a responsible entity to identify, classify, respond to, and report cybersecurity incidents related to critical cyber assets.

- CIP-009, **Recovery Plans for Critical Cyber Assets:** Requires the establishment of recovery plans for critical cyber assets using established business continuity and disaster recovery techniques and practices.

1.1.3.3 Information Systems and Information Security

National Institute of Standards and Technology (NIST) Special Publication (SP) 800-53, Recommended Security Controls for Federal Information Systems, was originally developed to provide guidance for securing traditional government-operated IT systems against cyber threats. However, NIST 800-53 has been used in nongovernment, as well as government-operated, IT and control systems environments.

In addition to issuing early cybersecurity guidelines, NIST is also contributing to the ongoing initiative to develop a unified information security framework. The framework is designed for the Federal Government and its contractors, and includes security controls for both national security and non-national security systems. Additional information pertaining to these efforts is provided in Appendix 3, Information Security Framework.

1.1.4 Dams Sector Authorities

Key authorities for the Dams Sector include the Tennessee Valley Authority Act of 1933, the Federal Power Act of 1920, the Dam Safety Act of 2006, the Water Resources Development Act of 2007, the Federal Mine Safety and Health Act of 1977, the Homeland Security Act of 2002, the Critical Infrastructure Information Act of 2002, and HSPD-7. Additional details on these authorities and others are presented in Appendix 4.

1.2 Dams Sector Critical Infrastructure and Key Resources Partners

Many of the processes and organizations established by the National Dam Safety Program were adapted and enhanced to accommodate the new and/or evolving relationships that developed from interdependencies with the Dams Sector. Communication, coordination, and collaboration with private and local government dam owners and operators are a vital component of these processes.

The Coordinating Councils for the Dams Sector are the primary mechanisms that DHS uses to establish and enhance relationships among all of the Dams Sector CIKR partners. A more complete description of the coordinating councils is provided in chapter 8.

The NIPP envisions CIKR partnerships as a framework to accomplish the following:

- Exchange ideas, approaches, and lessons learned;
- Facilitate planning and resource allocation for CIKR protection and resilience;
- Establish effective coordinating structures among partners;
- Enhance coordination with the international community; and
- Build public awareness.

The individual Dams Sector CIKR partners are described in the following subsections. The number and scope of the sector partnerships expanded as the sector matured since the issuance of the original DSSP in 2007.

1.2.1 U.S. Department of Homeland Security

As established by the Homeland Security Act of 2002 and HSPD-7, DHS provides a unifying core for the national network of organizations and institutions involved in efforts to secure the Nation's CIKR. DHS is responsible for leading, integrating, and coordinating the overall national effort to enhance CIKR protection; developing and implementing comprehensive, multi-tiered risk management programs and methodologies; generating cross-sector and cross-jurisdictional protection guidance, guidelines, and protocols; and recommending risk management and performance criteria and metrics within and across sectors. In addition to the direct involvement of the SSA as described below, several components within DHS have multiple responsibilities that contribute substantially to the protection and resilience of the Dams Sector.

The Federal Emergency Management Agency (FEMA) is the lead agency for the National Dam Safety Program and has worked for years with Federal and State agencies and private owners on implementing dam safety requirements and supporting initiatives. FEMA coordinates improvements to State dam safety programs by providing grants, supporting training and research initiatives, and coordinating better communication and public awareness. FEMA also conducts flood mapping for the Nation in its role as the administrator of the National Flood Insurance Program; its maps establish appropriate risk zone determinations behind levees for flood insurance purposes.

The United States Coast Guard (USCG) mission to provide maritime transportation safety, security, and mobility aligns with the navigation aspects of the Dams Sector. Many of the protective systems that USCG developed in its national defense role are transferable to some of the sector's most critical assets.

1.2.2 Sector-Specific Agency

The SSA Executive Management Office, within DHS IP, represents the designated SSA for the Dams Sector. The SSA works with DHS and the GCC to implement the NIPP sector partnership model and risk management framework, and to develop protective programs, resilience strategies, and related requirements. The SSA collaborates with private sector partners and encourages the development of appropriate voluntary information-sharing and analysis mechanisms within the sector.

In addition to managing the overall process for building partnerships, additional SSA responsibilities include the following:

- Identifying, prioritizing, and coordinating Federal activities in support of CIKR protection and resilience;

- Coordinating, facilitating, and supporting comprehensive risk assessment and risk management programs for high-risk assets and systems;

- Identifying sector-wide protection and resilience priorities;

- Incorporating protection activities as a key component of the all-hazards approach to domestic incident management within the sector;

- Facilitating the sharing of real-time incident notification, as well as CIKR protection recommended practices and guidelines;

- Promoting CIKR protection education, training, and awareness across the sector;

- Supporting dependency, interdependency, consequence, and other sector analyses; and

- Coordinating with DHS, the U.S. Department of State, and other appropriate departments and agencies to integrate U.S. CIKR protective programs into the international and global markets.

Additional SSA responsibilities are described in Section 2.2 of the NIPP.

1.2.3 Private Dams Sector Owners and Operators

A majority of the dams in the United States are privately owned and operated; 65 percent (more than 53,000) of the dams listed in the 2007 NID fall into this category. The number of privately owned levees is presently unknown; implementation of the proposed National Levee Database should rectify that problem. Most of the mine tailings and industrial waste impoundments are privately owned.

The SSA leverages existing relationships to work with private owners and operators to protect the sector's infrastructure. The goal of the SSA is to work with private owners and operators to implement sustainable protective programs and effective resilience strategies through information sharing and a variety of collaborative efforts. Interaction among the private and Federal and State governmental sectors is crucial to protecting sector assets.

1.2.4 Other Federal Departments and Agencies

Several Federal departments and agencies have important roles in the Dams Sector as owners, operators, or regulators of sector assets or because of dependencies or interdependencies with the Dams Sector. The following are active members of the GCC.

1.2.4.1 U.S. Department of Agriculture

The U.S. Department of Agriculture (USDA) is a major planner, designer, financier, constructor, owner, and/or regulator of more than one-third of all the dams in the United States that are included in the NID. USDA dams provide livestock water, municipal water, wastewater management, electric power, flood protection, irrigation, fish and wildlife habitat, recreation, sediment detention, and manure storage and treatment.

As a major component within USDA, the Natural Resources Conservation Service (NRCS) designs, finances, and constructs systems under its technical and financial assistance programs for individuals, groups, organizations, and governmental units for the purposes of water storage, sediment detention, and flood protection. Although the NRCS does not own, operate, maintain, or regulate any dams, it provides technical and financial assistance for almost 27,000 NID-sized dams[12] and financial assistance for more than 11,000 of them. The total number of levees constructed with NRCS support is presently unknown; most are

---

[12] A NID-sized dam must be more than 25 feet high or have an impounding capacity for maximum storage of 50 acre-feet or more.

designed to provide 4-percent (25-year) protection to support agricultural land use. The Forest Service within USDA owns approximately 1,000 NID-sized dams and administers permits for approximately 2,000 privately owned NID-sized dams.

1.2.4.2 U.S. Army Corps of Engineers

An element of the U.S. Department of the Army within the U.S. Department of Defense, USACE has responsibility or jurisdiction for dams that it planned, designed, constructed, and operates; dams that it designed and constructed, but are operated and maintained by others; and non-USACE dams and reservoir projects subject to Section 7 of the Flood Control Act of 1944, the Federal Power Act of 1920, as amended, and other laws for which it is responsible for prescribing regulations for the use of storage allocated to flood control and/or navigation. In addition, USACE has been involved with the dams for which it issues permits under its regulatory authority, as well as dams that USACE inventoried and inspected under the National Dam Inspection Act of 1972, the Dam Safety Act of 1986, and the National Dam Safety Program Act of 1996; however, USACE has no continuing responsibility or jurisdiction for those dams.

USACE is responsible for owning and/or operating 236 lock chambers at 192 sites; operating and maintaining 12,000 miles of inland and intracoastal waterways, and 13,000 miles of deep draft navigation channels; and owning and operating 653 dams and 75 hydropower projects with 350 generating units. More than 2,000 Federal levee systems are under USACE authorities, totaling more than 14,000 miles of infrastructure. In addition to civil works facilities, USACE provides dam safety support and technical assistance to the U.S. Army, U.S. Navy, and U.S. Air Force; the U.S. Department of Defense has more than 300 dams located on military facilities within the United States and its Territories.

USACE also provides technical and direct assistance to communities at risk from or affected by floods, through the provisions of Public Law 84-99, Flood Control and Coastal Emergencies. Under these provisions, USACE is authorized to undertake activities such as disaster preparedness, emergency operations (flood response and post-flood response), rehabilitation of flood control works threatened or destroyed by flood, protection or repair of federally authorized shore protective works threatened or damaged by coastal storm, and provision of emergency water due to drought or contaminated sources. Public Law 84-99 also allows for "advance measures" assistance to prevent or reduce flood damage conditions of imminent threat of unusual flooding. In addition, USACE is the lead agency for executing Emergency Support Function 3, Public Works and Engineering. Activities within the scope of this function include conducting pre-incident and post-incident assessments of public works and infrastructure; executing emergency contract support for life-saving and life-sustaining services; providing technical assistance to include engineering expertise, construction management, and contracting and real estate services; providing emergency repair of damaged public infrastructure and critical facilities; and implementing and managing the FEMA Public Assistance Program and other recovery programs.

1.2.4.3 U.S. Department of the Interior

As the Nation's principal conservation agency, the U.S. Department of the Interior (DOI) is responsible for most of the federally owned public lands and natural resources. DOI is responsible, through its bureaus, for the planning, design, construction, operation, oversight, and maintenance of nearly 3,000 dams. DOI's Working Group for Dam Safety and Security addresses dam-specific issues for the various DOI bureaus described below:

• The Bureau of Reclamation is a Federal water resource management and development bureau authorized to operate in 17 Western States. In carrying out its mission, the bureau developed water resource projects where dams play a major role in the viable development of the resources; 10 million acres of farmland are irrigated by Bureau of Reclamation water. The bureau maintains 479 dams and 348 reservoirs. The bureau also maintains several levees, such as the Colorado River channel, the Colorado River Front Work and Levee Project, and levees from Parker Dam to the U.S.-Mexico border.

• The Bureau of Indian Affairs works with American Indian Tribes and Tribal Nations to operate and maintain 859 dams on Indian reservations, 126 of which are classified as having high- and significant-hazard potential.

- The Bureau of Land Management (BLM) is responsible for agency-owned dams on public lands in 11 Western States, including Alaska. The BLM inventory consists of 590 dams, 8 of which are classified as having high-hazard potential.

- The U.S. Fish and Wildlife Service (FWS) operates facilities associated with fish and wildlife conservation on National Wildlife Refuges, waterfowl production areas, and national fish hatcheries. FWS has an inventory of 193 dams.

- The National Park Service has stewardship of 79 million acres of national parks and maintains 505 dams.

- The Office of Surface Mining oversees dams under its authority as Federal regulators under the Surface Mining Control and Reclamation Act of 1977, but does not own any dams. It oversees 73 dams, 8 of which are classified as having high-hazard potential and 12 of which are classified as having significant-hazard potential.

1.2.4.4 U.S. Department of Labor

The U.S. Department of Labor (DOL) has Dams Sector responsibilities under the Federal Mine Safety and Health Act of 1977 for dams constructed by the mining industry. The act specifically includes "impoundments, retention dams, and tailing ponds as part of a coal or other mine." The mining industry constructs dams for waste disposal, water supply, water treatment, and sediment control.

The DOL's Mine Safety and Health Administration is responsible for regulating the safety of mining industry dams. Mining-related dams are inspected as part of a full mine inspection that occurs four times per year for underground mines and twice per year for surface mines. It regulates 626 dams through its 11 Coal Mine Safety and Health Districts, and 1,903 dams through its 6 Metal and Nonmetal Mine Safety and Health Districts.

1.2.4.5 U.S. Department of State

The U.S. Department of State has a role in the Dams Sector through IBWC, which is composed of a U.S. Section and a Mexican Section, and has jurisdiction over two large international dams, four small diversion dams on the Rio Grande, and one small diversion dam on the Colorado River.

The U.S. Section is also responsible for the maintenance of several other dams and river control structures that are not fully international in nature. IBWC owns, operates, and maintains more than 500 miles of levees and associated floodways along the lower portion of the Rio Grande.

1.2.4.6 Federal Energy Regulatory Commission

FERC is authorized by the Federal Power Act to issue licenses to individuals, corporations, States, and municipalities to construct, operate, and maintain dams, water conduits, reservoirs, powerhouses, transmission lines, or other project works that are necessary for the development of non-Federal hydroelectric projects on navigable streams, public lands of the United States, and streams over which Congress has jurisdiction under the Commerce Clause of the U.S. Constitution, or that use surplus water or power from any Federal dam. FERC has jurisdiction over approximately 2,600 dams.

1.2.4.7 Tennessee Valley Authority

TVA is authorized by the Tennessee Valley Authority Act of 1933 to approve plans for the construction, operation, and maintenance of all structures affecting navigation, flood control, or public lands or reservations in the Tennessee River System. TVA is responsible for the planning, design, construction, operation, and maintenance of its 49 dams.

1.2.4.8 U.S. Department of Energy

The U.S. Department of Energy (DOE) is the designated SSA for the Energy Sector pursuant to HSPD-7 and is responsible for coordinating the protection of critical energy assets and assisting Federal, State, and local governments with disruption preparation, response, and mitigation activities. The agency is also the lead office for executing Emergency Support Function 12, which is an integral part of the larger DOE responsibility of maintaining continuous and reliable energy supplies for the Nation through preventive measures and restoration and recovery actions. The agency therefore has a natural affinity with the hydroelectric component of the Dams Sector. In addition, DOE owns and has jurisdiction over 15 dams at three sites.

1.2.4.9 Bonneville Power Administration

The Bonneville Power Administration is a Federal agency that serves the Pacific Northwest by operating an extensive electricity transmission system. It, along with the Southeastern, Southwestern, and Western Area Power Marketing Administrations, markets wholesale electrical power at cost from Federal and non-Federal dams, but does not own or have jurisdiction over them. Cumulatively, the power administrations serve 41 States.

1.2.4.10 National Weather Service

The National Weather Service (NWS), a component of the National Oceanic and Atmospheric Administration of the U.S. Department of Commerce, is the Federal agency authorized to issue hydrologic forecast and flash flood/flood warnings. During normal operations, NWS provides dam and levee operators with information that they can factor into their operations and planned discharges. During flood emergencies, NWS disseminates warnings to the public and local authorities for the purpose of saving lives and property. The agency also issues forecasts and warnings for hurricane landfall, flooding, flash-flooding, and river levels, all of which are of vital importance to dam, levee, and lock owners and operators, and downstream communities.

1.2.4.11 U.S. Environmental Protection Agency

EPA is responsible for protecting the water systems that depend on the water stored by dams or conveyed by canals. The agency is also the SSA for the Water Sector.

1.2.5 State Agencies

State governments have primary responsibility for protecting their populations from dam failure; they have regulatory responsibility for more than 70,000 (84 percent) of the 82,642 dams in the 2007 NID. Although programs vary in the scope of their authority from State to State, program activities typically provide for (1) safety evaluations of existing dams, (2) reviews of plans and specifications for dam construction and major repairs, (3) periodic inspections of construction of new dams or at existing dams, and (4) review and approval of emergency action plans (EAPs).

As described in Section 1.2.8, State agencies with jurisdiction over dams and levees are represented on the GCC. State efforts to regulate dams to ensure public safety began after the failure of the St. Francis Dam in California in 1928, the second worst U.S. dam failure after the Johnstown, Pennsylvania, failure of 1889.

The failure of the St. Francis Dam led to the enactment of legislation in California that became the model for laws in other States. By the mid-1970s, about half of the States had systems for protecting the public from the potential hazards of dams. Today, all States but Alabama have adopted dam safety regulatory laws.[13]

The Dam Safety Act of 2006 provides assistance to enhance State programs through grants and technical research and training. This program allows States to identify their own priorities and take appropriate action within the constraints of available resources. Funds provided annually through grants to State dam safety programs can be used by States to develop dam security vulnerability screening tools and threat response plans for dams with high-hazard potential. State assistance under the National Dam Safety Program is intended to help States bring the necessary resources to bear on inspection, classification, and emergency planning for dam safety. For a State to qualify for assistance under the 2006 act, State appropriations must be budgeted to

---

[13] The Alabama Department of Economic and Community Affairs, Office of Water Resources, is supporting the establishment of an Alabama Dam Security and Safety Program. The legislation to establish this program has been under development for several years.

carry out the State's legislation, and the State dam safety program must be working toward meeting the criteria in the act. With the exception of Alabama, States are meeting all or most of the act's criteria listed below:

- Review and approve plans and specifications to construct, enlarge, modify, remove, and abandon dams;

- Perform periodic inspections during dam construction to ensure compliance with approved plans and specifications;

- Give State approval upon completion of dam construction and before operation of the dam;

- Require or perform an inspection at least once every 5 years of all dams and reservoirs that would pose a significant threat to human life and property in case of failure in order to determine the continued safety of the dams and reservoirs, and require a procedure for more detailed and frequent safety inspections;

- Require that all inspections be performed under the supervision of a State-registered professional engineer with experience in dam design and construction;

- Issue notices, when appropriate, to require owners of dams to perform the necessary maintenance or remedial work, revise operating procedures, or take other actions, including breaching dams when necessary;

- Establish regulations for carrying out the State's legislation;

- Provide funds to ensure timely repairs or other changes to or removal of a dam to protect human life and property, and if the owner of the dam does not take the action described above, take appropriate action as expeditiously as possible;

- Institute a system of emergency procedures to be used if a dam fails or if the failure of a dam is imminent; and

- Identify each dam whose failure could be reasonably expected to endanger human life, the maximum area that could be flooded if the dam failed, and public facilities that would be affected by the flooding.

The Nation does not yet have an equivalent of the National Dam Safety Program for levees. In a 2006 survey, only 23 States reported that they have some degree of regulatory authority or responsibility over levees. In those States, levee oversight could be the responsibility of State floodplain management programs or the dam safety office.

Congressional impetus to develop the National Dam Safety Program arose from several dam failures in the 1970s. Similarly, hurricanes Katrina and Rita in 2005 spurred Congress to pass the National Levee Safety Act[14] and task the Committee on Levee Safety to develop recommendations for a national levee safety program. The committee's draft recommendations for a national levee safety program are listed in Section 1.2.7.

1.2.6 Relationship with the National Dam Safety Program

As the lead agency for the National Dam Safety Program, FEMA worked for years with other Federal and State agencies and private industry on implementing requirements and initiatives for dam safety. FEMA was established in 1979 by Executive Order 12148 in response to the need for unified and coordinated efforts for Federal assistance in national disasters. Executive Order 12148 also provided that the Director of FEMA would coordinate all Federal efforts in dam safety. In 1986, Title XII of the Water Resources Development Act was enacted to establish and maintain dam safety programs, including training for dam safety inspectors. Ten years later, the Water Resources and Development Act of 1996 codified a program that had been successfully promoting dam safety and mitigating the effects of dam failures for more than 20 years. Section 215 of the 1996 act formally established the National Dam Safety Program and named the Director of FEMA as its coordinator. The passage of the 1996 act represented the culmination of years of collaborative efforts by the dam safety community to statutorily create the National Dam Safety Program.

---

[14] The National Levee Safety Act is Title IX of the Water Resources Development Act of 2007.

The National Dam Safety Review Board (NDSRB) and the Interagency Committee on Dam Safety (ICODS) play an important role in guiding the National Dam Safety Program and coordinating efforts across the dam safety community. Both organizations are chaired by FEMA and were reauthorized under the Dam Safety Act of 2006.

1.2.6.1 National Dam Safety Review Board

The NDSRB provides the Director of FEMA with advice in setting national dam safety priorities and considers the implications of national policy issues affecting dam safety, assists FEMA in the review of State dam safety programs, and establishes reasonable costs for implementing a State dam safety program. The NDSRB is composed of 11 voting members representing the departments of Agriculture, Defense, and the Interior; FEMA; FERC; five members from State dam safety offices; a member representing the private sector; and a nonvoting representative from the DOE national laboratories.

1.2.6.2 Interagency Committee on Dam Safety

The Interagency Committee on Dam Safety encourages the establishment and maintenance of effective Federal programs, policies, and guidelines to enhance dam safety, and serves as the permanent forum for the coordination of Federal activities in dam safety. ICODS is composed of representatives from Federal agencies that build, own, operate, or regulate dams, and currently includes members representing the departments of Agriculture, Defense, Energy, Interior, and Labor, as well as FEMA, FERC, the Nuclear Regulatory Commission, TVA, and the IBWC–U.S. Section.

1.2.7 National Committee on Levee Safety

The following are among the draft recommendations from the National Committee on Levee Safety that encompass levee safety at the Federal and State levels. Many of these recommendations are consistent with those made in a draft 2008 white paper developed from a series of meetings convened by the SSA of a panel of levee experts representing owners, professional organizations, and the insurance industry. The Dams Sector supports the formation of a National Levee Safety Program and implementation of the following recommendations:

- Establish a National Levee Safety Commission to provide national leadership and comprehensive and consistent approaches to levee safety, including standards; R&D; technical materials and assistance; training; public involvement and education; collaboration on environmental and safety issues; facilitation of the alignment of Federal programs; and the design, delegation, and oversight of a delegated program to the States.

- Expand and maintain the National Levee Database to include a one-time USACE inventory and inspection of all non-Federal levees to include baseline information useful in understanding critical safety issues, the true costs of good levee stewardship, and the state of individual levees to facilitate risk-informed decisionmaking.

- Adopt a hazard classification system as the first step in identifying and prioritizing hazards in leveed areas.

- Develop and adopt national levee standards that assist in ensuring that the best engineering practices are available and implemented throughout the Nation at all levels of government.

- Develop tolerable risk guidelines to facilitate the understanding of options to reduce risks and the role of uncertainty in risk assessments, better inform levee construction/enhancement decisions, and weigh nonstructural alternatives to flood risk management in a risk-informed context.

- Change the term "levee certification" to "compliance determination" to more clearly articulate the intent that "certification" under the National Flood Insurance Program requirements does not constitute a safety guarantee or warranty.

- Develop a comprehensive national public involvement and education/awareness campaign to communicate risk and change behavior in leveed areas.

- Provide comprehensive technical materials and direct technical assistance to support successful implementation of consistent national standards to the States, local communities, and owners and operators.

- Develop a National Levee Safety Training Program to increase the level of expertise and knowledge in all aspects of levee safety.

- Develop and implement measures to more closely harmonize levee safety activities with environmental protection requirements to ensure that critical levee operations and maintenance are not delayed.

- Conduct an R&D program to continually advance state-of-the-art techniques and practices for levee safety and the conduct of critical operations and maintenance activities in as cost-effective and environmentally friendly a manner as possible.

- Design and delegate safety program responsibilities to the States to assist State and local governments in developing effective safety programs focused on continual and periodic inspections, emergency evacuation, mitigation, public involvement, and risk communication and awareness.

- Establish a Levee Safety Grant Program to assist the States and local communities in developing and maintaining the institutional capacity, necessary expertise, and program framework to quickly initiate and maintain levee safety program activities and requirements.

- Establish the National Levee Rehabilitation, Improvement, and Flood Mitigation Fund to aid in the rehabilitation, improvement, or removal of aging or deficient national levee infrastructure.

- Explore potential incentives for good levee behavior through alignment of existing Federal programs.

- Mandate the purchase of risk-based flood insurance in leveed areas to reduce economic flood damages and increase individuals' and communities' understanding that levees do not eliminate the risk of flooding.

- Augment FEMA's mapping program to improve risk identification and communication in leveed areas and consolidate critical information about flood risk.

- Align FEMA's Community Rating System to reward development of State levee safety programs by providing further incentives to communities to exceed minimum program requirements and benefit from lower risk-based flood insurance rates for policy holders who live in leveed areas.

1.2.8 Relationships with State, Local, Tribal, and Territorial Governments

State governments are responsible for regulating 84 percent of dams on the current NID list. Because of this important role, States are represented in the sector through the participation of eight State dam safety officials on the GCC. These GCC members, from geographically diverse areas, represent the interests of all State dam safety officials to the sector. These members also established a State Dam Security Panel to address a wide range of State dam security issues, as well as to offer training, technical workshops, and other CIKR protection and resilience products to enhance technical security expertise throughout the sector.

Local governments, public utilities, levee districts, and water management districts own and operate dams and levees. The interests of these owners and operators are represented on the SCC and LSCC by their fellow owners and operators and by professional organizations such as the Association of State Dam Safety Officials (ASDSO), the National Hydropower Association, the Association of State Floodplain Managers (ASFPM), and the National Association of Flood and Stormwater Management Agencies (NAFSMA). The complete list of SCC and LSCC members is provided in Section 8.3.

Non-Federal governments are also represented in the Dams Sector through liaison with the State, Local, Tribal, and Territorial Government Coordinating Council (SLTTGCC). Members of the council are invited to participate in all quarterly meetings of the Dams Sector's councils and the SSA and SLTTGCC representative conducts periodic conference calls to ensure maximum exchange of information.

In addition to the inclusion of tribal government interests in the sector through the SLTTGCC liaison, the Bureau of Reclamation, a GCC member, represents the Bureau of Indian Affairs, which operates 859 dams on Indian lands. In addition, it maintains overall Safety of Dams program responsibility and works with the Indian tribes and tribal nations to operate and maintain those dams. Working with the tribes to protect and develop natural resources on their reservations is an important Federal trust responsibility.

1.2.9 Relationships with Private Sector Organizations

Private national and international dam safety organizations have significant connections with and influence on the Dams Sector. The ASDSO, ASFPM, NAFSMA, the National Hydropower Association, the National Mining Association, the National Water Resources Association, The Infrastructure Security Partnership (TISP), and the United States Society on Dams (USSD) play important roles in coordinating and contributing to sector safety, security, and resilience.

Levees, for example, are an important element of many State floodplain management programs. Local governments are the foundation of comprehensive floodplain management because they are generally responsible for planning, determining, and supervising the use of land within their jurisdictions. Furthermore, they are often the impetus for obtaining financial and technical assistance from State and Federal agencies to reduce flood losses. However, local governments may be limited in their work with levees and levee owners because of limited legal authority and technical expertise, and budget constraints. ASDSO, ASFPM, and NAFSMA perform valuable education, training, and outreach services for these levee owners.

1.2.9.1 Association of State Dam Safety Officials

ASDSO is a national, nonprofit organization of State and Federal dam safety regulators, dam owners and operators, and others interested in promoting dam safety. It has approximately 2,800 members. Many of the State dam safety officials who are members also have some degree of regulatory authority for levee safety in their State. ASDSO has taken a firm position on supporting the development of national and State levee safety programs.

1.2.9.2 Association of State Floodplain Managers

ASFPM is an organization of professionals involved in floodplain management; flood hazard mitigation; the National Flood Insurance Program; and flood preparedness, warning, and recovery. ASFPM represents the flood hazard specialists of Federal, State, and local governments; the research community; the insurance industry; and the fields of engineering, hydrologic forecasting, emergency response, water resources, and others. The mission of ASFPM is to promote education, policies, and activities that mitigate current and future losses, costs, and human suffering caused by flooding, and to protect the natural and beneficial functions of floodplains—all without causing adverse impacts. The safety and resilience of levees and dams are of great interest to floodplain managers.

1.2.9.3 National Association of Flood and Stormwater Management Agencies

NAFSMA, an organization of State and local public agencies whose functions are the protection of lives, property, and economic activity from the adverse impacts of storm and flood waters, has a natural linkage to the Dams Sector. The association advocates public policy, encourages the use of technologies, and conducts educational programs that facilitate and enhance the achievement of the public service function of its members.

1.2.9.4 National Hydropower Association

The National Hydropower Association is a nonprofit national association committed exclusively to representing the interests of the hydroelectric power industry. Its members represent more than 61 percent of domestic, non-Federal hydroelectric capacity in the United States. The association's membership consists of more than 140 companies, including public utilities, investor-owned utilities, independent power producers, equipment manufacturers, environmental and engineering consultants, and attorneys.

1.2.9.5 National Mining Association

The National Mining Association is a nonprofit trade association that provides a forum in which the diverse segments of the mining industry come together to advocate public policies designed to protect and expand opportunities for domestic mining. Association members include more than 325 corporations involved in all aspects of the mining industry, including coal, metal and industrial mineral producers, and mineral processors. The association's connections to the Dams Sector are the mine tailings and other industrial waste impoundment constituencies.

1.2.9.6 National Water Resources Association

The National Water Resources Association is a nonprofit federation of State organizations whose membership includes rural water districts, municipal water entities, commercial companies, and individuals. The association's concerns with the appropriate management, conservation, and use of water are directly related to the interests of the Dams Sector.

1.2.9.7 The Infrastructure Security Partnership

TISP was established after the September 11th attacks as a forum in which U.S.-based public and private sector nonprofit organizations collaborate on issues involving the resilience and security of the Nation's built environment regarding natural and manmade disasters. TISP facilitates dialogue on critical infrastructure resilience issues across multiple sectors by leveraging the technical expertise from public and private stakeholders, including design, construction, and engineering consulting firms. TISP membership currently includes more than 180 organizations.

1.2.9.8 United States Society on Dams

USSD, formerly the U.S. Committee on Large Dams, was established in the early 1930s and is the nationwide professional organization focusing on dam and water resources development. USSD represents the United States as one of the 83 member countries of the International Commission on Large Dams and has served as the private sector member of the NDSRB since its establishment in 1998.

1.2.9.9 Other Relevant Organizations

Many other national and international groups also have potential interests in Dams Sector issues:

- American Consulting Engineers Council
- American Public Works Association
- American Society of Civil Engineers
- Associated General Contractors of America, Inc.
- Earthquake Engineering Research Institute
- Electric Power Research Institute
- Floodplain Management Association
- International Association of Emergency Managers
- National Emergency Management Association
- National Governors Association
- National Society of Professional Engineers

- National Watershed Coalition

- Natural Hazards Research and Applications Information Center

- North American Electric Reliability Council

- Portland Cement Association

1.2.10 International Relationships

In the aftermath of the September 11th attacks, the Canadian, Mexican, and U.S. governments focused attention on their shared borders. In December 2001, Canada and the United States signed the Smart Border Declaration, which includes a 32-point action plan, to promote legitimate travel and commerce across the U.S.-Canadian border while protecting both countries from crime and terrorism. In March 2002, the United States signed a similar accord with Mexico that included a 22-point action plan that outlined specific actions to determine and address security risks while expediting the flow of legitimate goods and people across the U.S.-Mexican border.

Since 2005, the leaders of Canada, Mexico, and the United States have been meeting annually at the North American Leaders' Summit. Among the areas of focus for trilateral cooperation are safe and secure borders and facilitation of legitimate flows of goods and travelers, to ensure both the safety of the citizens of North America and the continent's economic competitiveness.

1.2.10.1 United States and Mexico

The Critical Infrastructure Protection Framework Agreement between Mexico and the United States provides the basis for the safe, efficient, and secure operation of the international dams on the countries' borders. Consistent with the agreement, the countries conduct joint inspections of the international dams on a five-year schedule. Corrective actions for deficiencies identified during these inspections are addressed in a risk-based priority order.

In addition to the five-year inspections, the countries conduct joint annual security assessments of their shared critical infrastructure. They also work cooperatively to develop strategies to secure the international diversion and storage dams. The countries alternate conducting silt surveys to determine the reservoir capacities at the Amistad and Falcon International Storage Dams; these studies are done on a ten-year basis.

1.2.10.2 United States and Canada

Many rivers and some of the largest lakes in the world lie along or flow across the border between the United States and Canada. These lakes and rivers are used for many purposes in both nations, which at times results in conflict.

The International Joint Commission (hereinafter referred to as "the commission") was established by the 1909 Boundary Waters Treaty. The commission has six members—three appointed by the President of the United States, with the advice and approval of the Senate, and three appointed by the Governor General in the Council of Canada, on the advice of the Prime Minister. The commissioners adhere to the treaty as they prevent or resolve disputes. More than 20 boards, made up of experts from the United States and Canada, help the commission carry out its responsibilities. The commission rules on applications for the approval of projects affecting boundary or transboundary waters and may regulate the operation of these projects; assists the two countries in protecting the transboundary environment, including the implementation of the Great Lakes Water Quality Agreement; and alerts the governments on emerging issues along the border that may give rise to bilateral disputes.

In cases such as approving applications for dams or canals, the commission authorizes uses while protecting competing interests in accordance with the rules established by the two governments. If it approves a project, the commission can set conditions limiting water levels and flows (e.g., to protect shore properties and wetlands and the interests of farmers, shippers, and others). After a structure is built, the commission may continue to play a role in how it is operated. There are 15 dams under the jurisdiction of the commission.

The International Commission on Large Dams (ICOLD) is an international organization that comprises representatives from the National Committees on Dams from 86 different participating countries. ICOLD provides a forum for the exchange of knowledge and experience in all aspects related to dams, leading the profession in ensuring that dams worldwide are built and operated safely, efficiently, economically, and without detrimental effects on the environment. ICOLD hosts annual meetings and congresses (every 3 years) that continuously build on the experiences gained at previous ICOLD meetings to actively advance the state of the practice in all aspects of dam operations and water management.

1.3 Dams Sector Goals and Objectives

Figure 1-3: Establishing Goals and Objectives

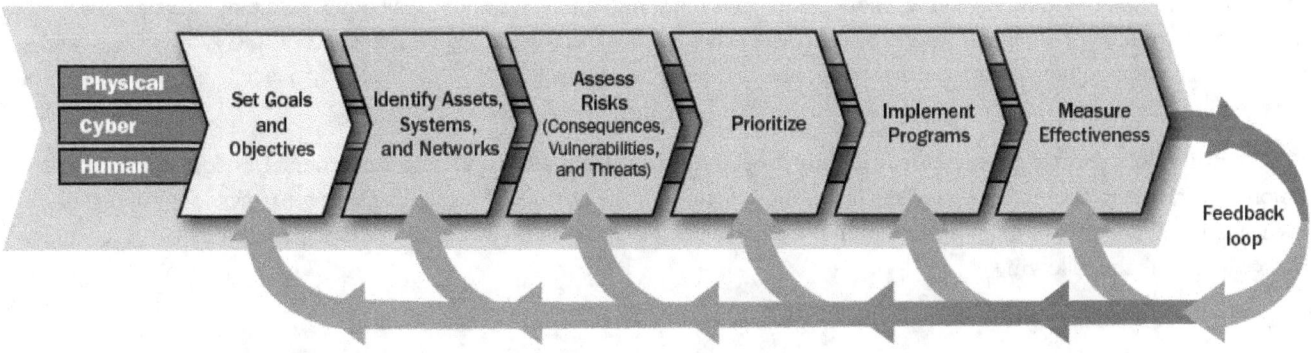

Continuous improvement to enhance protection of CIKR

1.3.1 Elements and Characteristics of Dams Sector Goals and Objectives

An effective Dams Sector partnership is instrumental in building and achieving a common vision shared by sector asset owners and operators. The vision statement forms the basis for sector-specific goals and objectives that collectively represent a safe, secure, and resilient posture. The Dams Sector goals are based on the following vision statement:

> The Dams Sector will identify the measures, strategies, and policies appropriate to protect its assets from terrorist acts and enhance their capability to respond to and recover from attacks, natural disasters, or other emergencies through the development of multi-faceted, multi-level, and flexible protective programs and resilience strategies designed to accommodate the diversity of this sector. The Dams Sector, by fostering and guiding research in the development and implementation of protective measures and resilience-enhancing technologies, will ensure the continued economic use and enjoyment of this key resource through a risk-informed management framework addressing preparedness, response, mitigation, and recovery.

The entire risk management framework for the DSSP is intimately linked to the Dams Sector's vision, goals, and objectives, which are a logical, complementary component of the NIPP. Risk reduction is achieved through the successful, coordinated implementation of sustainable protective programs and effective resilience strategies. The overall benefits of the proposed risk management framework are maximized when these programs and strategies are designed and implemented to address risk reduction from an all-hazards perspective.

The Dams Sector goals and objectives are driven by a desire to establish an effective risk management framework across the sector. The remaining sections describe how the sector works toward accomplishing these goals.

1.3.2 Process to Establish Sector Goals and Objectives

The Dams Sector goals and supporting objectives were developed through a consensus of representatives from the SSA and the sector councils, and reflect the overall risk management outcomes that owners, operators, and government officials collectively seek as strategic direction for the Dams Sector.

1.3.3 Dams Sector Goals and Objectives

The following eight goals and supporting objectives developed by the CIKR partners in concert with the SSA reflect the desired future status of physical, cyber, and human elements for the Dams Sector. These goals and objectives support the overarching goal of the NIPP: "[To b]uild a safer, more secure, and more resilient America by preventing, deterring, neutralizing, or mitigating the effects of deliberate efforts by terrorists to destroy, incapacitate, or exploit elements of the Nation's CIKR, and to strengthen national preparedness, timely response, and rapid recovery of CIKR in the event of an attack, natural disaster, or other emergency."

Goal 1: Build Dams Sector partnerships and improve communications among all CIKR partners. Developing a common vision and achieving a safe, secure, and resilient infrastructure for the Dams Sector requires strong partnerships among all owners and operators. Communication within these partnerships is vital to their effective operation. The objectives for meeting this goal include the following:

- Establish robust and active sector councils as cornerstones for the sector partnership model;

- Obtain and maintain security clearances for all appropriate sector partners; and

- Establish mechanisms for coordination and rapid dissemination and exchange of information, including R&D results, lessons learned, and effective CIKR protection and resilience practices.

Goal 2: Identify Dams Sector composition, consequences, and critical assets. Baseline information describing sector composition and landscape is needed to assess the relative importance of assets within the sector. Identification of critical elements is performed through a systematic, consequences-based screening. The objectives for meeting this goal include the following:

- Develop, support, and maintain comprehensive inventories of sector assets;

- Develop the required criteria and conduct systematic screening to identify critical assets within the Dams Sector;

- Develop an effective program to characterize critical assets; and

- Develop protocols and schedules for collecting and updating critical asset information.

Goal 3: Improve the Dams Sector's understanding of viable threats. Inherent in reducing risks is the need to understand the threats to sector assets. Threat information not only contributes to the risk assessment process, but also plays an integral part in determining overall protective program strategies and ultimately dictates proper protective measures. The objectives for meeting this goal include the following:

- Increase awareness of the threat environment across the Dams Sector;

- Increase information reporting and sharing among asset owners, operators, regulators, and key personnel tied to the emergency response; and

- Identify and communicate Dams Sector-specific threats, including physical, cyber, and human elements.

Goal 4: Identify Dams Sector vulnerabilities. Risk reduction can be achieved through a clear understanding of asset vulnerabilities. The objectives for meeting this goal include the following:

- Promote awareness and assist asset owners and operators with vulnerability assessments, as requested;
- Identify Dams Sector-specific physical, cyber, and human vulnerabilities; and
- Increase information sharing among CIKR partners regarding generic and emerging vulnerabilities.

Goal 5: Identify the risks to Dams Sector critical assets. Risks are a function of the threat type, critical asset vulnerabilities, and the resulting consequences. The objectives for meeting this goal include the following:

- Develop a sector-wide conditional risk assessment framework to identify high-risk (the most critical) assets within the Dams Sector;
- Develop protocols and schedules for updating information regarding the most critical assets; and
- Compare risk information across the most critical assets within the Dams Sector to determine priorities.

Goal 6: Develop guidance on how the Dams Sector will manage risks. After Dams Sector risks have been identified and prioritized, guidance will be necessary to assist sector owners and operators in managing them. The objectives for meeting this goal include the following:

- Support implementation of protective programs and resilience strategies; and
- Develop guides and reference documents to manage the risks and support technical transfer, outreach, and training on readiness, response, protection, and recovery issues.

Goal 7: Enhance the security and resilience of the Dams Sector through R&D efforts. R&D efforts are an important component in reducing the risks to the Dams Sector. The objectives for meeting this goal include the following:

- Identify the R&D needs and requirements of the Dams Sector;
- Identify ongoing and planned relevant R&D by Dams Sector CIKR partners and other sectors; and
- Improve coordination and share the results associated with relevant R&D initiatives to optimize the benefits across the Dams Sector.

Goal 8: Identify and address interdependencies. The Dams Sector does not exist and perform its overall missions independently from the other infrastructure sectors identified in the NIPP. For example, power generation is vital to the Energy Sector; municipal and irrigation water is vital to the Water Sector. The objectives for meeting this goal include the following:

- Develop and implement collaborative efforts to identify intra- and cross-sector interdependencies; and
- Develop multi-jurisdictional exercises and regional pilot programs to assess the impacts of interdependencies, define effective mitigation strategies, and enhance disaster resilience.

1.4 Value Proposition

The full engagement of Dams Sector CIKR partners in developing and implementing protective programs depends on understanding the benefits that can accrue to their operating environment through participation in sector activities. Sector partners can benefit by receiving information on potential threats; exchanging information; having access to tools that assess facility risk; and obtaining guidance that explains how to detect, deter, mitigate, or respond to risks.

The SSA and its sector partners will minimize the resources required to implement an effective sector-wide risk management framework by focusing on protective programs and resilience strategies that are as follows:

- Simple to implement, with low cost and high effectiveness;

- Consistent with effective practices and shared among stakeholders using industry and trade association communication mechanisms;

- Based on cost-sharing incentives, market systems, and other means that would encourage private sector participation;

- Built on current practices that have been proven to be effective;

- Applicable across assets while allowing owners and operators to select the most appropriate method for the particular need;

- Reliant on self-assessments, where appropriate; and

- Consistent with the risk profile and commensurate with the threat environment from an all-hazards perspective.

All asset owners and operators are urged to participate in the activities of the sector, communicate activities to the appropriate representatives, and express their concerns to sector leaders who can advise them of the appropriate channels to follow for problem resolution. Through these means, the overall protection and resilience of the Dams Sector will be enhanced.

2. Identify Assets, Systems, and Networks

Figure 2-1: Identifying Assets, Systems, and Networks

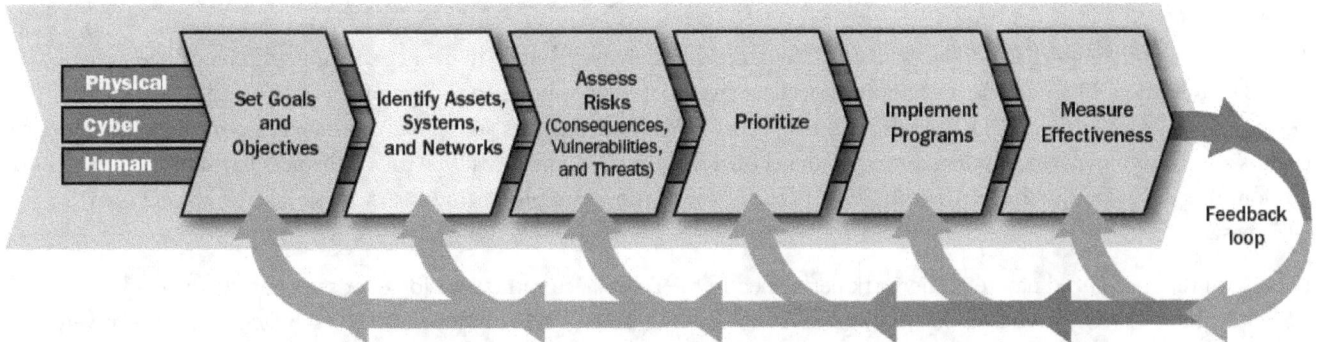

Continuous improvement to enhance protection of CIKR

This chapter describes the mechanisms used to gather basic information on sector assets, as well as the processes that may be used to identify or screen the critical assets within the sector. The characterization of sector assets and the development of a comprehensive inventory of critical assets that can then be further analyzed with respect to vulnerabilities and protective actions are required to achieve the goals and objectives identified in chapter 1.

2.1 Defining Information Parameters

This section describes the important information parameters in the Dams Sector. It describes the National Inventory of Dams and the National Levee Database, and presents the sector taxonomy.

2.1.1 Definition of Relevant Information Parameters

The information parameters that are relevant to the Dams Sector include the sector assets' physical structures, cyber infrastructure, personnel needs, and security configurations. The multiplicity and complexity of sector asset functions dictates the importance of these elements as described below.

2.1.1.1 Physical Elements

Dams in the United States range in height from a few feet to more than 700 feet, and in length from a few tens of feet to more than 1 mile. Normal reservoir storage (i.e., the volume of water stored in a reservoir for a majority of the time) behind U.S. dams can range from a few acre-feet to 30 million acre-feet. Dams in the U.S. Territories range from 30 feet to 274 feet high, with reservoir sizes that range from 100 acre-feet to 55,000 acre-feet. Dams are also located near or along the borders with Canada and Mexico.

In addition to the main impounding structure, one or several appurtenant structures may be associated with the multiple purposes of the facility. Examples of the types of structures that could be appurtenant to a dam include free overflow and gated spillway structures, outlet works, water supply features, penstocks, power generation features, navigation locks, embankments associated with the main structure (also known as saddle dams, dikes, and freeboard dams), and different types of control structures. Each dam type and each appurtenant structure has its own purpose and varying degrees of vulnerability. In general, each functional component may be associated with different protective configurations.

Levees (and flood risk reduction systems in general) may feature multiple components, including embankment sections, as well as floodwall sections, pumps and pumping stations, interior drainage works, flood damage reduction channels, closure structures, penetrations (e.g., utilities and pipes), and transitions (i.e., sections where the materials constituting the levee system change from, for example, a conventional floodwall section to an earthen section).

2.1.1.2 Human Element

The safe operation and security of the Nation's CIKR depend heavily on the human element. Sector facilities can be either staffed or unstaffed. Many smaller or remote assets have minimal requirements for operation and can be operated without personnel onsite for fairly lengthy periods of time (e.g., a week). Some facilities are operated remotely from central operations centers and may or may not require on-site personnel on a daily basis. Some are staffed on a "business day schedule" (i.e., 8- or 10-hour schedules for 5 to 7 days a week). Some of the larger or more complex facilities require staff to be present on a 24/7 basis.

Because of the specialized nature of the work performed in the Dams Sector, the workforce for sector assets such as hydro-power facilities or navigation locks has considerable stability compared to other industries, and each facility has a relatively small workforce. As such, asset owners are well acquainted with their workers and schedules. As a consequence, the potential for criminal infiltration is very limited in that impostors or infiltrators or insider threats would be easier to recognize than is the case for other types of infrastructure. In addition, due to this smaller and more easily recognized workforce, the work environment is significantly easier to monitor and unusual activity, such as surveillance, terrorist attacks, and other criminal activities, is much easier to distinguish and respond to in the early stages of a potential situation. However, this may not be necessarily applicable to other types of facilities, such as levees, for example, which are spatially distributed and require easy and open access for maintenance purposes.

The number of personnel required to operate and maintain a dam can vary significantly. The need for staff depends greatly on the complexity of the asset and the benefits derived from it. Larger hydropower dams may require adjustments in operations several times per hour to respond to generation needs and economics. They may require several operators for each shift; a crew of maintenance and monitoring personnel; specialized staff that respond to hourly, daily, or weekly adjustments to power demands; marketing specialists; transmission line crews; and security personnel and guards. Simple, less complex facilities may require only one person to operate the structure and perform monitoring and maintenance duties. For example, recreational dams and stock ponds have minimal staffing needs. Staffing at levees and flood control projects is somewhat similar to that at dams, but is more focused on operations and maintenance activities and will vary depending on water levels and weather conditions.

Many of these positions are highly technical and specialized in nature and require personnel with three or more years of apprentice work or advanced training. Operations at some dams may also require the use of either the full-time or corporate sharing of management and IT personnel. Personnel succession plans and continuity-of-operations plans help to ensure ongoing operation in the event of work stoppages and extended periods of illness, such as during pandemics. In addition, the schedule for noncritical operations can be modified to respond to situations that may be understaffed (e.g., establishing a deferred maintenance schedule).

2.1.1.3 Cyber Element

Industrial control systems assist in the efficiency and safety of dam operations and maintenance and play a key role in many sector facilities. Control systems vary widely on the basis of age and generation of the system; thus, they also vary with respect to complexity and sophistication. Some systems are closed systems and use isolated networks, as well as proprietary communication protocols, while others use open architectures, common communication paths, and rely on the Internet. In addition, control systems at dams may also be connected to the electric power grid. Most dam owners, if not all, use various computer security methods for master terminal units, data servers, and historians, such as authentication procedures, encryption, firewalls, anti-virus software, and anti-spyware.

Many of the industrial control systems used today were designed for operability and reliability during an era when security received low priority. These systems operated in fairly isolated environments and typically relied on proprietary software, hardware, and/or communications technology. Infiltrating and compromising these systems often required specific knowledge of individual systems architecture and physical access to system components.

In contrast, newer control systems are highly network-based and use common and open standards for communication protocols, such as Internet Protocol addressable. Many controllers are Internet Protocol addressable. Asset owners and operators have gained immediate benefits by extending the connectivity of their systems and have increasingly adopted commercial off-the-shelf technologies that provide the higher levels of interoperability required among today's modern infrastructure. Standard operating systems such as Windows or UNIX are increasingly used in central supervisory stations, which are now typically connected to remote controllers via public-private networks provided by telecommunications companies. Common telecommunications technologies, such as the Internet, public-switched telephone networks, or cable or wireless networks, are often used.

As a general proposition, levee operations are conducted by smaller entities and are considerably less dependent on information technology than dams. They rely on basic telecommunications and information infrastructures that can be supplemented with manual operations.

2.1.1.4 Security Configuration Characteristics

The Dams Sector contains unique characteristics that have an important influence on the implementation of security measures. First, the spatial dimensions of dam projects are significantly larger than those of the facilities within other sectors. Second, there are often multiple components that are critical for project purposes that are non-adjacently located. Each one of these components may be potentially associated with different security configurations. Third, many dams are located in remote areas; thus, a response force belonging to local law enforcement authorities may take longer to arrive once an alarm is received. For some attack types, the appropriate response may not arrive in time to thwart the attempt. Finally, most dams have no armed guard forces.

The security configuration of sector assets may include a combination of features, such as fences and gates, vehicle-resistant perimeters, boat barriers, intrusion detection systems, electronic entry control systems, closed-circuit televisions (CCTVs), appropriate lighting, patrols and guards, and hardening of select components.

In addition to these electronic and physical security features, Dams Sector partners also rely on robust security plans that define operational security procedures, such as information protection; threat and suspicious incident analysis centers; planned, scaled responses to varying threat levels; and coordination with law enforcement agencies. Owners and operators test EAPs to help protect populations at risk and maintain response and recovery plans to bring project benefits back online rapidly.

2.1.2 National Inventory of Dams

Congress authorized USACE to inventory dams in the United States with the National Dam Inspection Act of 1972. The NID was first published in 1975, and has since been periodically updated. The Water Resources Development Act of 1986 authorized USACE to maintain and periodically publish an updated NID; the Dam Safety Act of 2006 reauthorized periodic updates and provided a continued funding mechanism.

The NID contains the most current information on the Nation's dams and represents a very successful partnership among the States, Territories, and Federal agencies. It is a dynamic, online database with scheduled and periodic interim updates as improved data are received from participants. The NID features Internet-based tools to query the data and a geographic information system interface that allows for data display and analysis. On the basis of the 2007 NID update, the United States and the U.S. Territories of Guam and Puerto Rico reported 82,642 dams that meet NID criteria.

All dams designated as having high-hazard potential or significant-hazard potential are to be included in the NID. Low-hazard or undetermined potential classification dams that either (1) equal or exceed 25 feet in height and which exceed 15 acre-feet in storage, or (2) equal or exceed 50 acre-feet storage and exceed 6 feet in height are also to be included in the NID. The NID does not include levees, some navigation locks, canal structures, some types of industrial waste impoundments, or hurricane barriers.

From a safety perspective, it is common to classify dams according to the potential impact that a failure or an operational error would have on upstream and/or downstream areas or at locations remote from the dam. *The Federal Guidelines for Dam Safety: Hazard Potential Classification Systems for Dams* (FEMA 333)[15] provides simple definitions to characterize downstream hazard potential. Table 2-1 lists the parameters outlined in FEMA 333.

Table 2-1: Dam Safety Hazard Potential Classifications (FEMA 333)

Hazard Potential Classification	Loss of Human Life	Economic, Environmental, Lifeline Losses
Low	None expected	Low, generally limited to owner
Significant	None expected	Yes
High	Probable, one or more expected	Yes, but not necessary for this classification

The 2007 version of the NID lists 11,881 dams with high-hazard potential classifications, 13,549 dams with significant-hazard potential classifications, and 57,194 dams with low-hazard potential classifications.

2.1.3 Dams Sector Taxonomy

A basic taxonomy was developed for the Dams Sector that identifies four main categories representing families of assets or types of systems with distinct characteristics. Table 2-2 provides a summary of this taxonomy.

---

[15] Federal Emergency Management Agency, *Federal Guidelines for Dam Safety: Hazard Potential Classification Systems for Dams*, FEMA 333, October 1998 (reprinted April 2004).

Table 2-2: Dams Sector Taxonomy

Category	Segment	Examples of Components
Dam Projects ("Dams") As special cases, it includes the following: Navigation Projects Hydropower Projects	Water Retention Structures	· Embankment Section · Concrete Section
	Water Control Structures	· Spillway · Outlet Works
	Impoundments	· Reservoir
	Hydropower Facilities	· Conventional Plant · Run-of-the-River Plant · Pumped Storage Plant
	Navigation Structures	· Navigation Lock
	Water Transmission Structures	· Canal
	Operation and Control Facilities	· Remote Operation Facility · Control Center
	Public Access Facilities	· Visitor Center · Parking
Flood Damage Reduction Systems ("Levees")	Flood Protection Structures	· Levee · Flood Wall · Dike
	Water Control Structures	· Pumping Station · River Control Structure
	Water Transmission Structures	· Canal
Hurricane and Storm Surge Protection Systems	Structural Protection Systems	· Hurricane Barrier · Dike · Shoreline Protection Structure · Levee
	Non-Structural Protection Systems	· Wetlands
Mine Tailings and Industrial Waste Impoundments	Impoundment Retention Structures	· Impounding Structure
	Impoundment Control Structures	· Spillway · Outlet Works
	Impoundments	· Tailings · Industrial Waste Residuals

2.2 Collecting Infrastructure Information

Collecting the information needed to coordinate a national strategy for the security, protection, and resilience of the Dams Sector requires a truly collaborative effort among CIKR partners. Owners and operators hold asset information. Appropriate processes must be developed to encourage and facilitate voluntary data submittals and address information protection concerns.

The protection of submitted information is a major concern for the private sector. Private owners need unmitigated assurance that their more sensitive data will not be shared outside DHS without prior approval from the owner of the data under every conceivable scenario, and that, if released without permission, actionable penalties will result. The failure to establish appropriate protective mechanisms for private sector information may represent an insurmountable obstacle to the successful implementation of a truly national strategy for CIKR protection.

Although the NID is an effective data collection system and is the primary method for maintaining general data on conventional dam structures, dam owners are under no regulatory requirement to submit data to the NID.

The Consequence-Based Top-Screen (CTS) methodology provides another effective avenue for the consolidation of important information pertaining to sector assets. The purpose of this methodology is to systematically assemble consistent data that can be used to identify the sector's critical assets (i.e., those high-consequence assets whose failure or disruption could potentially lead to the most severe impacts at a national or sector level). The potential consequences are considered through a number of parameters that quantify the impacts or effects associated with failure or disruption of the project. These parameters provide a characterization of human impacts, economic impacts, and impacts on critical functions.

2.2.1 Data Collection Processes

The following sections describe the data collection process for the NID, the CTS, and the National Levee Database.

2.2.1.1 NID Data Collection Process

The first step in the process of transmitting information to the NID requires each Federal or State agency to develop a candidate submittal database management file. This file is designed to consistently consolidate required inventory items. The NID contains 60 fields, some of which are optional for the States and some of which are designated for Federal agency use only. Table 2-3 provides the NID fields used for data collection.

Table 2-3: National Inventory of Dams Fields Used for Data Collection

1. Dam Name	16. Owner Type	31. Normal Storage	46. Length of Locks
2. Other Dam Name(s)	17. Dam Designer	32. Surface Area	47. Lock Width
3. Dam Former Name	18. Non-Federal Dam on Federal Property	33. Drainage Area	48. Permitting Authority
4. State or Federal Agency ID	19. Dam Type	34. Downstream Hazard Potential	49. Inspection Authority
5. NID ID	20. Core	35. Emergency Action Plan	50. Enforcement Authority
6. Number Separate Structures	21. Foundation	36. Inspection Date	51. State Jurisdictional Dam
7. Other Structure ID	22. Purposes	37. Inspection Frequency	52. State Regulatory Agency
8. Longitude	23. Year Completed	38. Condition Assessment	53. Federal Agency Involvement in Funding
9. Latitude	24. Year Modified	39. Condition Assessment Detail	54. Federal Agency Involvement in Design
10. Section, Township, Range Location	25. Dam Length	40. Condition Assessment Date	55. Federal Agency Involvement in Construction
11. County	26. Dam Height	41. Spillway Type	56. Federal Agency Involvement in Regulatory
12. River or Stream	27. Structural Height	42. Spillway Width	57. Federal Agency Involvement in Inspection
13. Nearest City/Town	28. Hydraulic Height	43. Outlet Gates	58. Federal Agency Involvement in Operation
14. Distance to Nearest Downstream City/Town	29. Maximum Discharge	44. Volume of Dam	59. Federal Agency Owner
15. Owner Name	30. Maximum Storage	45. Number of Locks	60. Federal Agency Involvement—Other

The USACE Topographic Engineering Center developed and deployed software to help State and Federal dam owners and regulators compile, manage, and report NID data through the process depicted in Figure 2-2. The Dam Safety Program Management Tools (DSPMT) desktop software enables data owners to review inventory changes, correct mistakes, and easily send inventory updates to USACE. The use of this software results in the receipt of more consistent data and correct inventory codes, which enables resolution of discrepancies among data owners. The States and some Federal agencies also use this software for other reporting purposes to simplify data reporting.

Most States and Federal agencies use the DSPMT to add information to their own databases, link NID fields to their own data fields, and check for errors. The DSPMT also enables users to send an electronic NID submittal automatically, which is the preferred method of data collection.

The Dams Sector clearly has the components for an efficient data collection process for dams. Efforts are continually focused on refining the NID to facilitate its use by the States and Federal partners; USACE has worked closely with Federal agencies and with ASDSO to update and publish the NID. One of the most important results of a 30-year national program in dam safety is that the sector is collecting basic data on conventional dams at frequent intervals.

Figure 2-2: Flow of Information to the National Inventory of Dams

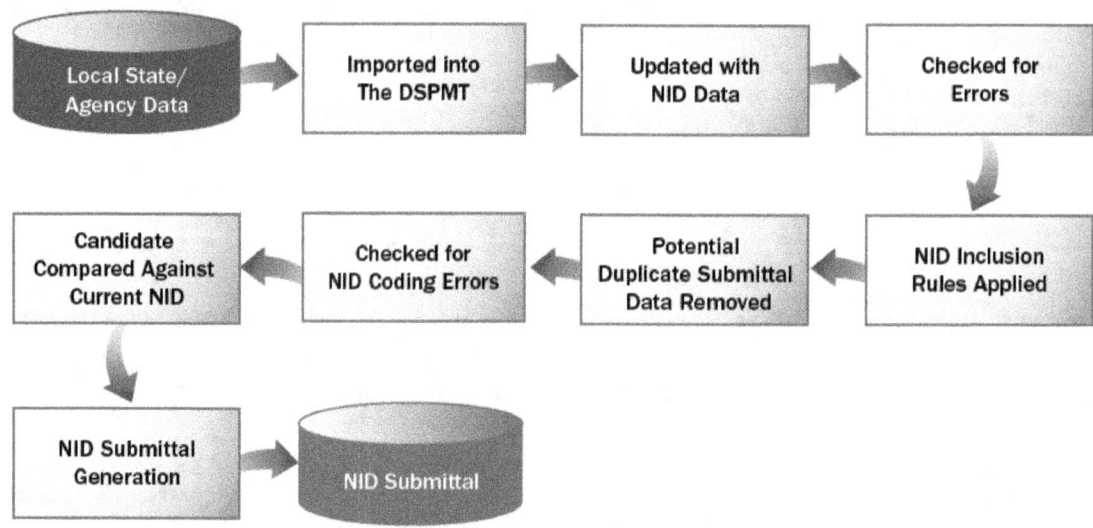

2.2.1.2 CTS Data Collection Process

The CTS methodology is a quick screening approach that can be used to effectively identify and characterize the subset of high-consequence facilities within the Dams Sector whose failure or disruption could potentially lead to the most severe impacts. The CTS process is implemented through an interactive Web-based questionnaire that addresses general facility, contact, and consequence information. This methodology is described in Section 3.2.

The CTS data fields that correspond to general facility information include several of the NID data items, as well as some additional data fields related to project operations and characteristics. Many fields in this section are pre-populated with the NID data.

The contact information section includes the facility point of contact (owner/operator representative(s) qualified to answer technical questions about project characteristics and its different operations). Finally, the consequence section focuses on a number of parameters that are used as part of the CTS screening and prioritization process. These parameters, such as population at risk (PAR), are consistent with the general consequence categories established by the NIPP. The CTS methodology focuses on the following potential impacts resulting from severe damage or disruption of the facility: human impacts (the impacts on human health and safety caused by inundation of downstream populated areas, industrial areas, and other critical infrastructure assets), economic impacts (the impacts associated with damages to the facility, direct damage to downstream inundated areas, and direct monetary impacts associated with lost project benefits), and impacts on critical functions (the secondary effects associated with the disruption or loss of the critical functions provided by the facility). The CTS questionnaire includes a number of tables that allow users to select, from pre-established ranges, the appropriate values that are applicable to the facility. Table 2-4, Consequence-Based Top-Screen Parameters, depicts the consequence categories and parameters, and measurement units used in the CTS methodology.

Table 2-4: Consequence-Based Top-Screen Parameters

Consequence Category	Consequence Parameter	Measurement Unit
Human Impacts	Total Population at Risk (PAR)	Number of people
	PAR 0–3 miles	Number of people
	PAR 3–7 miles	Number of people
	PAR 7–15 miles	Number of people
	PAR 15–60 miles	Number of people
Economic Impacts	Asset Repair/Replacement Cost	Millions of dollars
	Remediation Cost	Millions of dollars
	Business Interruption Cost	Millions of dollars/year
Impacts on Critical Functions	Water Supply: Population Served	Number of people
	Irrigation: Annual Water Deliveries	Millions of dollars/year Acre-feet/year
	Hydropower Generation: Total Installed Capacity	Megawatts
	Flood Damage Reduction: Annual Damages Prevented	Millions of dollars/year
	Inland Navigation: Annual Navigation Tonnage	Kilotons/year
	Recreation: Annual Recreational Visitors	Number of people/year

2.2.1.3 Levee Data Collection Process

The National Levee Safety Act of 2007 requires USACE to develop a database to include the location information of the Nation's federally owned and operated levees. The database is to also include those levees that were federally constructed but are non-federally operated and maintained and those levees that were not federally constructed but have subsequently been enrolled in the USACE Rehabilitation and Inspection Program.

The database is to contain, based on available information, the general condition of each levee and an estimate of the number of structures and the population at risk and protected by each levee that would be adversely impacted if the levee fails or is breached. The geospatial National Levee Database will include the necessary attributes of levees and floodwalls relevant to design, construction, operations, maintenance, repair, inspections, and the potential for failure. The National Committee on Levee Safety recommends the expansion of the National Levee Database to include a one-time USACE-conducted inventory of all non-Federal levees. The development and implementation of the CTS for levees will leverage the information gathered through these efforts and consolidate the consequence parameters required for the identification of those critical levees associated with the highest potential consequences.

2.2.2 Data Collection Gaps

Although the NID provides the Dams Sector with an extremely useful and efficient tool for identifying and collecting basic data on dams, a number of important gaps exist in the information needed to fully quantify the consequence, vulnerability, and interdependency characteristics of individual assets and systems across the sector.

These include gaps in the sufficiency of data, resource availability, identification and characterization of unregulated dams and other sector assets and systems, and identification of cyber and human elements. A discussion of these gaps follows.

2.2.2.1 Gaps in the Sufficiency of Data

The NID captures a wealth of project-specific information on conventional dams in the United States that fit the NID definition of a "dam." However, some basic information required for detailed consequence and/or vulnerability assessments, including information on cyber and human elements, is not contained in the NID.

Dams listed in the NID are assigned a hazard potential classification rating that provides an indication of the potential consequences of a sudden, catastrophic dam failure. These ratings do not, however, indicate the likelihood of the failure or provide an adequate indicator of expected fatalities or economic consequences. Because some dams are designed for flood control purposes only and can represent a high-hazard potential only during extreme floods, it is impossible to distinguish relative importance among projects in the high-hazard category. Portfolio screening tools require some additional variables, such as downstream population at risk, and this information is collected through the CTS.

Federal and State agencies appear to use various levels of standards in quantifying the potential consequences associated with dam failure. In most cases, it appears that the secondary impacts resulting from dam failure are not addressed in great detail (e.g., inundation of a factory may be identified as a consequence, but the loss to the entire local economy due to the loss of the factory may not be). Use of a sector-wide approach to quantify consequences would certainly result in consistency and would facilitate a comparison of the results.

Some of the current data gaps are a logical consequence of the NID's focus on dam safety. The broader definition and scope of the Dams Sector and the larger number of different assets that it comprises may require additional data collection and consolidation efforts to fully identify and characterize the sector. A potential initiative could involve maximizing the data integration and consolidation benefits provided by the NID and its associated data collection tools. As an example, the State Dam Security Panel has worked with USACE and ASDSO to introduce questions into the DSPMT that gauge the involvement of State dam safety officials in security issues at dams under their jurisdiction.

Other coordinated efforts could lead to recommendations for capturing the additional information elements needed to fully characterize a facility, such as freeboard characteristics, spillway and outlet works details, and data on cyber and human elements in addition to the physical descriptors. This information could be collected for sector-critical dams.

Additional data collection efforts should focus on surveying and cataloging other types of assets not necessarily included in the NID, such as mine tailings and other industrial waste impoundments, hurricane barriers, river control structures, and levees. These efforts should be developed by leveraging any related ongoing or planned Federal- or State-level initiatives, such as the proposed expansion of the National Levee Database to include a one-time inventory and inspection of all non-Federal levees.

The NID is generally updated every two years, thereby ensuring the relative currency of the information on dams that meet the criteria for NID listing. Information on the number of mine tailings impoundments under the jurisdiction of the Mining

Safety and Health Administration is readily available and is up-to-date. The currency of the information in the National Levee Database will depend on if and how often it will be updated.

2.2.2.2 Gaps in Resource Availability

Most agencies at the State level faced major challenges in allocating resources to support data collection even before being significantly impacted by current and projected future budget deficits. This lack of resources, for example, may inhibit States from providing USACE with location information on non-Federal levees, which could affect the thoroughness of the national levee inventory mandated by the National Levee Safety Act. Many States also lack the authority and resources required to evaluate the protective and resilience conditions of their jurisdictional dams, or to support any related data collection efforts.

As a basic principle, infrastructure assets must be appropriately maintained to remain safe and operationally reliable. Owners and operators are forced to balance the resources required for data collection initiatives related to protection and resilience with those requirements directly associated with safety, operation, and maintenance. Therefore, it is critically important to coordinate these multiple data collection requirements as much as possible to alleviate the corresponding burden.

2.2.2.3 Gaps in Data for Unregulated Dams and Other Sector Assets

Another data collection challenge relates to the identification of unregulated dams and other sector assets and systems. Gaps include the number of unregulated dam-type structures that fall outside the definition of a NID dam (e.g., some navigation locks, levees, canals, and other similar water retention and control structures) and the number of dams that have not been classified correctly.

NDSRB established a Performance Measures Task Group to develop standard definitions for reporting State-regulated dams to the NID and to other databases. NDSRB should consider broader issues related to capturing information on all types of dams, including mine tailings dams at abandoned mines that are not State-regulated, other industrial waste impoundments, and dams that are not regulated but that meet the definition of a dam in the NID.

2.2.2.4 Gaps in Identification of Cyber Information

As the primary data consolidation platform for dams, the NID was not designed originally to capture cyber-related information, such as hardware, software, networks, and critical information and data. This information is also critical to enhancing the sector's understanding of cyber threats, vulnerabilities, and corresponding dependencies/interdependencies. Therefore, an effective mechanism must be developed by the sector to collect basic data on cyber elements related to critical dams. Depending on the case, a series of basic data items could be collected initially; for example, whether there are any specific control systems that are critical to the project missions. This could be implemented as part of a sector-wide characterization of those critical assets identified by the initial screening. As noted earlier, levee systems are considerably less dependent on information technology and are therefore less vulnerable to cybersecurity issues. However, as the sector progresses in identifying critical levee systems, it will attempt to collect information on cyber elements in those systems.

2.2.2.5 Gaps in Human Asset Identification

The Dams Sector currently does not have a sector-wide mechanism to collect and analyze information related to the importance of the human element and its vital role in ensuring reliable and continuous operation of critical facilities. Some of the essential operating and management positions include dam operators (tenders); operation and maintenance personnel; safety engineers and inspectors/monitors/data collectors; specialized mission-critical personnel, such as power buyers, power distributors, and lock operators; security and protection professionals; supervisory/management personnel; and IT specialists.

Many of these positions are highly technical and require advanced training. In the absence of qualified personnel, some critical assets could be understaffed or improperly staffed. Forward-looking corporations, agencies, and other dam owners currently have robust personnel succession programs in place, others may not. Although not currently captured for the Dams Sector, the sector must begin collecting data on human elements related to critical facilities to determine if this is a viable concern.

2.3 Verifying Infrastructure Information

In the particular case of the NID, procedures are in place for verifying asset data submitted to the database. First, the NID has been automated to merge and compare data submitted by users on a record-by-record and field-by-field basis. Second, by performing data submittal workflows at the State and Federal agency levels with the DSPMT, those most familiar with the data and most qualified to make any changes—specifically data owners, managers, and data providers—are alerted by the program to any data that potentially needs attention, modification, or double-checking. Performing these workflows at the State and Federal agency levels and using the original data from the day-to-day dam inventory management tools significantly enhance data quality and the accuracy of the submittal. When discovered, errors in the data set are reported to the submitting agency, which then is responsible for making corrections. In addition, the CTS will provide a complementary mechanism for data verification by enabling additional access to the NID data fields and encouraging owners and operators to check the accuracy of the corresponding entries.

A process, yet to be identified, also will be established by the sector to verify any cyber and human element data to be collected for critical facilities. The process will include protocols similar to those discussed above for reviewing cyber and human data, steps to address incomplete and/or inaccurate data, follow-up criteria and activities, and special verification steps to account for the differences between cyber and human asset data and physical/people asset data.

It may be difficult to resolve issues regarding asset data verification procedures for those sector assets currently outside of safety regulation programs. To the extent possible and through engagement with local authorities, sector partners will actively attempt to be aware of the presence of unregulated assets to determine (1) if any may be critical to the Nation, and (2) if any need to be included in the list of critical sector assets.

2.4 Updating Infrastructure Information

Mechanisms shall be implemented for owners and operators to voluntarily participate in the updating of asset data on a regular basis. The updated data should be made available to the SSA so that Dams Sector CIKR partners will be able to leverage the most up-to-date data when making decisions concerning sector-wide protection and resilience strategies.

Infrastructure information is updated periodically in the NID, generally every two years, but updating is not to exceed an interval of 5 years. The objectives of the NID are the same as those stated in the 1989 ASDSO National Inventory of Dams Methodology:

- Update inventory data on dam-type structures with information from the States and Federal agencies;

- Foster State self-sufficiency through assistance for States to maintain and update their own inventory systems, and transfer the information to the NID;

- Obtain the participation of all States in the NID; and

- Maintain State control of the information submitted by those States.

In addition, exercises provide an excellent opportunity for updating infrastructure information and testing EAPs. Inundation maps based on multiple reservoir pool levels and different flood conditions also have been developed for many of the largest dams. Dam owners should perform an annual evaluation of the human development occurring downstream of their dams to identify and gather information on potentially affected populations and infrastructure. For those dams potentially associated with severe consequences that do not have detailed and up-to-date inundation studies, the Dams SSA will encourage their development by providing technical assistance and facilitating the use of inundation modeling tools.

The SSA, in close collaboration with the sector partners, will update the infrastructure data corresponding to sector critical assets through the annual implementation of the CTS data call. The corresponding Web-based tool will be expanded to include not only asset-specific information but also any relevant data at the system level, including infrastructure interdependencies and regional impacts.

2.5 Protecting Asset Data

A challenge that must be overcome in the Dams Sector relates to how sensitive project-specific critical asset data will be safeguarded. This challenge is a critical one in the area of Internet-provided data on sector assets. Chapter 8 provides additional discussion on information sharing and protection.

Following the September 11th attacks, USACE removed the NID from public access while it analyzed the ramifications of maintaining the open availability of NID information. The ICODS NID Subcommittee (now called the National Dam Safety Review Board Working Group on the NID) concluded that most of the NID data did not pose significant security risks to the Nation's dams and represented information that could be obtained by the public through other means. Access to the NID was restored, including a new Web site with enhanced capabilities. However, access to three data fields (hazard potential classification, nearest downstream city, and distance to nearest downstream city) is available only to government users. Public NID users can request this information from the corresponding dam regulatory agency.

The protection of sensitive information must be accomplished by taking into consideration the owner's right to safeguard information critical to its facilities and business operations, while also taking into account the potentially affected population's right to be aware of any significant health or safety risks. An effective risk communications strategy must balance these two requirements and gauge the most appropriate solution in order to maximize the benefits to all affected stakeholders. In some special cases, unrestricted release of sensitive information could actually increase the risk to downstream communities by making a high-consequence facility even more attractive for potential adversarial actions. In any case, a successful risk communications strategy must clearly define not only the "what" (What is the right type of information? Is it actionable and effective in mitigating risk?), but also the "how" (What is the best way to directly provide this information to the affected stakeholders?).

In some cases, the level of sensitivity resides in the systematic aggregation of information. For example, a specific data field in a database may not be sensitive as an individual piece of information, but data mining and database query processes may lead to sensitive results by aggregation. In addition, a comprehensive risk communications strategy should consider an all-hazards framework. The relative probability of the undesirable event should be taken into account in order to identify the most effective strategy for risk mitigation. For example, levee overtopping under significant flood conditions may be associated with a relatively higher probability of occurrence than a potential dam failure under extreme loading conditions; the potential sensitivity of any consequence information associated with seasonal events would be much lower than in the case of extreme events.

Technical details and engineering specifications regarding dams and appurtenant structures are regarded as sensitive and are given the designation "For Official Use Only" (FOUO) and "Critical Energy Infrastructure Information" by various Federal agencies. Such designations have protected sensitive information from Freedom of Information Act (FOIA) requests; nondisclosure agreements may be required prior to information release. The results of vulnerability assessments and security procedures and responses may or may not be classified, depending on the level of detail contained in those reports and the concerns of the asset owner.

The sharing of sensitive information among Federal agencies is common, but has been less so across Federal and State boundaries because of concerns about the ability of the individual States to protect sensitive information in light of their own "Sunshine Laws." The promulgation of the rule establishing the procedures for the DHS Protected Critical Infrastructure Information

(PCII) Program may alleviate information-sharing concerns.[16] Submitted sensitive information that satisfies the PCII requirements is protected from FOIA disclosure and State and local disclosure laws. Furthermore, it cannot be used in civil litigation or as the basis for a regulatory action. Nevertheless, DHS has indicated that there may be exigent cases (e.g., impending emergencies) where submitted information may be passed to organizations with a "need to know." This issue has raised concerns within the private sector and has yet to be addressed.

---

[16] *Federal Register*, Volume 71, September 1, 2006, p. 52262.

3. Assess Risks

Figure 3-1: Assessing Sector Risks

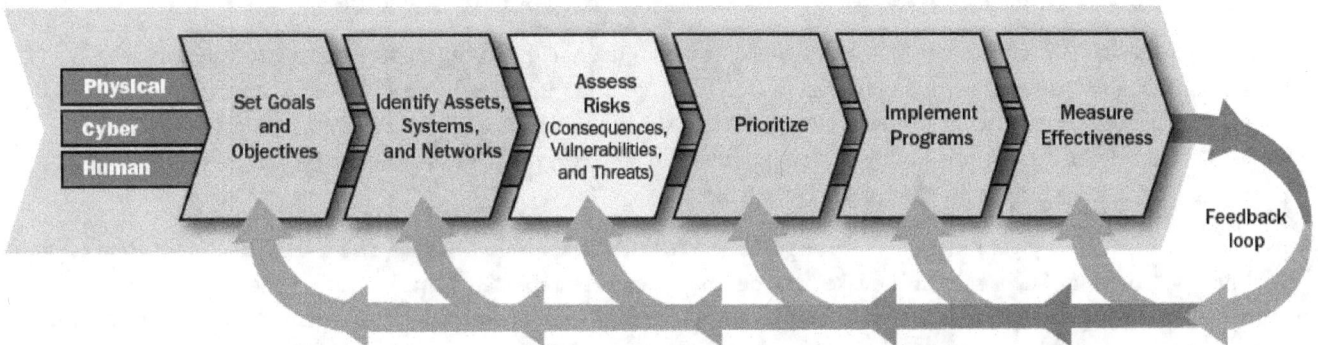

Continuous improvement to enhance protection of CIKR

The risk profile facing the Dams Sector arises from multiple sources, including natural disasters such as floods and earthquakes, structural deficiencies, aging infrastructure, accidents or equipment malfunctions, and deliberate aggressor actions. These risk sources could potentially lead to temporary disruption of critical functions or severe damage to and even structural failure of dams, levees, and their related assets. In the event of a dam failure and uncontrolled release of water, the potential energy of the water stored behind even a small dam is capable of causing loss of life and enormous property damage. The failure of some levees has the potential to cause immediate loss of life, as well as significant short- and long-term consequences.

Because most of the dams and levees in the United States are located in rural areas, they have not been a "high crime" target; in fact, most criminal activities associated with sector assets have been relatively minor, such as vandalism and theft. Moreover, because of their sturdy construction, dams historically have been unattractive targets for potential small-scale organized attack, although they have been very attractive targets for nation-states during times of war. Finally, because most dams are in rural locations, they do not provide the level of anonymity for surveillance or other precursor activities offered by an urban setting. Despite these facts, the Dams Sector recognizes that assets must be considered possible terrorist targets because such attacks at select sites have the potential to cause significant downstream casualties and economic losses.

In an all-hazards context, risks to levees can originate from unsafe conditions arising from improper maintenance, natural events that exceed design thresholds, and the actions of aggressors. The condition of many levees has not been assessed since they were constructed so there is limited understanding of their resilience. There is, however, a general understanding that levees could be considered targets of possible aggressors because terrorist attacks on select levees have the potential to cause significant casualties and economic losses, particularly in urban areas.

This chapter presents information on how the Dams Sector can identify more effectively its overall risk by detecting relevant threats and vulnerabilities so that appropriate protection and mitigation measures can be implemented.

3.1 Use of Risk Assessment in the Dams Sector

The Dams Sector has long-standing and well-established programs to assess, mitigate, and respond to the potential damages caused by catastrophic dam failures induced by natural hazards. The sector's levee community has also placed increased emphasis on safety as evidenced by the passage of the National Levee Safety Act in 2007 and the formation of the National Committee on Levee Safety.

The level of experience and body of knowledge developed by the dam and levee safety communities in the identification of structural and operational deficiencies with respect to the extreme demands imposed by natural hazards and the quantification of the consequences of potential failure are applicable to the risk assessment problem from the critical infrastructure protection perspective. Compiling the knowledge gained on deficiencies and vulnerabilities through safety and security programs provides a good basis for evaluating the risks associated with extreme events caused by terrorist activities.

The NIPP defines risk as a function of three parameters: (1) threat (the likelihood of an attack being attempted against the target); (2) vulnerability (the susceptibility of the target to being compromised by the attack, given that it is attempted); and (3) the consequences of the attack, if successful. Rigorous risk models consider the threat and vulnerability parameters as probabilities: Threat is defined as the probability of a given type of attack, and vulnerability is defined as the probability that a given type of attack against the target will be successful, if attempted.

This is consistent with the definition of risk corresponding to natural hazards. In this case, risk is defined as a function of the probability that an event, such as an earthquake or flood, may occur; the probability that the facility may not perform to the required performance level (e.g., a structural failure could be an example of unacceptable performance); and the corresponding consequences. A widely used approach defines risk as the product of these three variables, that is $R = T \times V \times C$, where R is risk, T is threat, V is vulnerability, and C is the consequences. For a given attack type, the conditional risk, R_c, is defined as the product of the vulnerability and the corresponding consequences. Figure 3-2 depicts these definitions.

Figure 3-2: Definition of Total and Conditional Risk

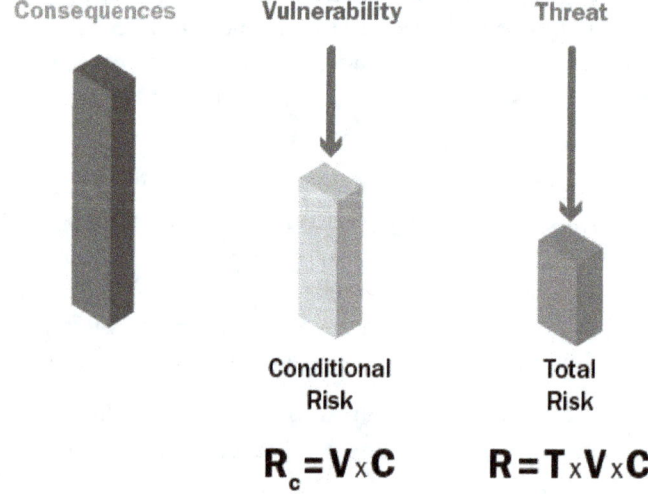

Many Federal and non-Federal agencies and companies with ownership or regulatory responsibility for dams in the Nation have strong, extensive backgrounds in developing and applying methodologies for assessing risk and prioritizing assets. On their own initiative, USACE, the Bureau of Reclamation, and TVA conduct comprehensive risk assessments at federally owned dams under their self-regulating authorities. Private and municipal hydroelectric utilities under the jurisdiction of FERC also complete mandatory vulnerability and security assessments at their critical facilities that are consistent with FERC and industry-developed security guidance. Hydroelectric utilities also comply with the risk-based assessments and annual cyber vulnerability requirements established by NERC.

Most dams in the Nation are State-regulated. Vulnerability assessment and prioritization activities for these dams are in the initial stages largely because, with the notable exception of a few States, no well-established, applicable regulatory framework exists. On the one hand, owners of these dam are reluctant to complete vulnerability assessments because they lack funding, regulatory drivers, or a sense of urgency. On the other hand, many of these dams do not represent viable terrorist targets. It is clear that a consistent approach is needed to assess actual sector-wide risks in a way that does not impose an artificial or unnecessary burden on the owners and their regulators.

The multiple risk assessment methodologies currently in use across the Dams Sector are well suited for owner use, but they are based on different assumptions and approaches, and generally do not follow a common terminology. Almost all security risk assessments address the consequence, vulnerability, and threat components of the problem; more often than not, they define and measure these variables in very different ways. There is little agreement on what factors are to be examined and how they are to be measured. This presents technical and logistical obstacles for sector-wide risk assessment efforts as it often results in unique solutions that cannot be easily compared. As a result, these methodologies, while extremely useful in their own right at the owner level for asset-specific analyses, cannot meet the requirements and expectations at the national and sector levels.

A sector-wide risk assessment approach must satisfy the need for a practical methodology that is suitable for comprehensive sector-wide use and must yield risk results that can be objectively compared across the sector. The desired sector-wide risk assessment model will make use of data from existing risk analyses, thus leveraging the efforts already being made by owners and operators through asset-specific assessments, with the goal of conducting a sector-wide prioritization without having to collect or develop significant amounts of new data. This sector-wide risk assessment model will strive for the lowest achievable complexity and logistical burden, while taking maximum advantage of existing assessments. The model needs to be simple, transparent, and easy to use, but also mathematically defensible and scalable to provide for more rigorous analyses, if needed.

There are three potential risk assessment levels, as presented in Figure 3-3:

- Asset-specific risk assessment;
- Sector-wide risk assessment; and
- Cross-sector risk assessment.

Figure 3-3: Risk Assessment Levels

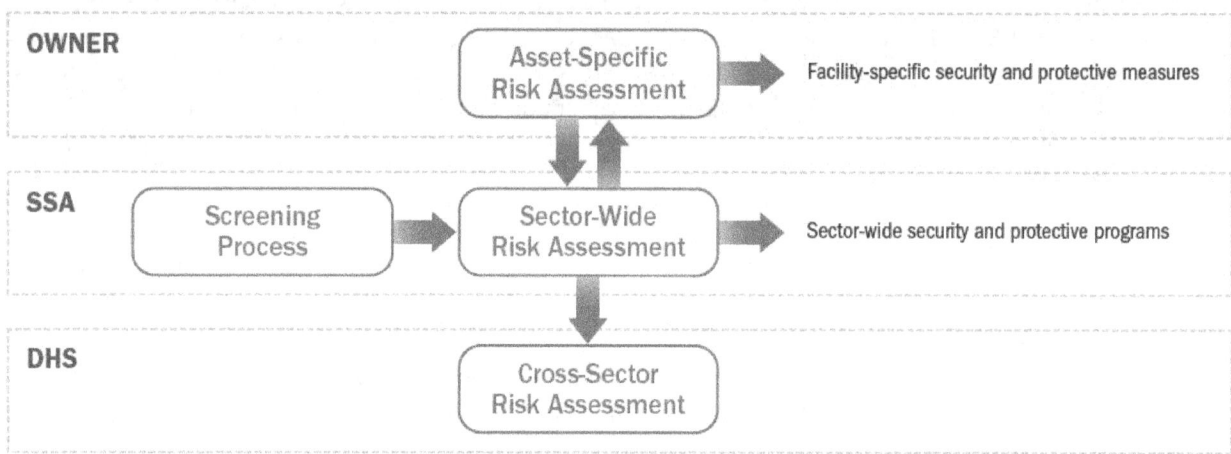

The asset-specific (or facility-specific) risk assessment is conducted by owners and operators and generates results that inform the design and implementation of site-specific protective programs. All risk assessments completed within the Dams Sector to date have been completed at this level; owners and operators have assessed their assets as a whole, including the appropriate cyber elements, if applicable. To the extent possible, these self-assessments have included project-specific consequence data; however, the scope of the consequence assessments varies widely.

The purpose of the sector-wide risk assessment is to generate results that characterize the risk profile for the entire sector. It must be noted that it is not necessary for every single facility within the sector to contribute to the composite risk picture since the sector profile will be mostly driven by those assets and systems that are potentially associated with the highest risks. The Dams SSA is responsible for leading and coordinating the development of this sector-wide assessment. Although this effort has not been completed, some sector partners are coordinating their efforts proactively to ensure consistency and/or similarity in future data collection or risk analysis initiatives, which will aid in the development of a sector-wide risk picture.

The Dams SSA actively seeks the voluntary collaboration of all CIKR partners to design a risk management framework that facilitates such a sector-wide assessment. A sector-wide assessment based on a conditional risk approach could offer extremely useful insight on the types of attacks that could affect large segments of the sector or its subsectors, or the types of assets that could be associated with the highest risk for specific attack vectors. The Dams SSA will work with all CIKR partners and request their input to develop a methodology that can be useful in supporting this effort within the sector. The active participation of CIKR partners in the development of a sector-wide conditional risk assessment effort (conceptually portrayed in Figure 3-4) is certainly critical in determining those obstacles and challenges that could limit its voluntary support by owners and operators as an effective approach for the sector. A key element for its successful development will be the ability to capitalize on existing information and incorporate the results from previous assessments whenever possible. The development and implementation of this sector-wide risk assessment does not duplicate or replace current requirements at the facility level and does not conflict with the need for facility-specific assessments.

Figure 3-4: Sector-Wide Risk Assessment Framework

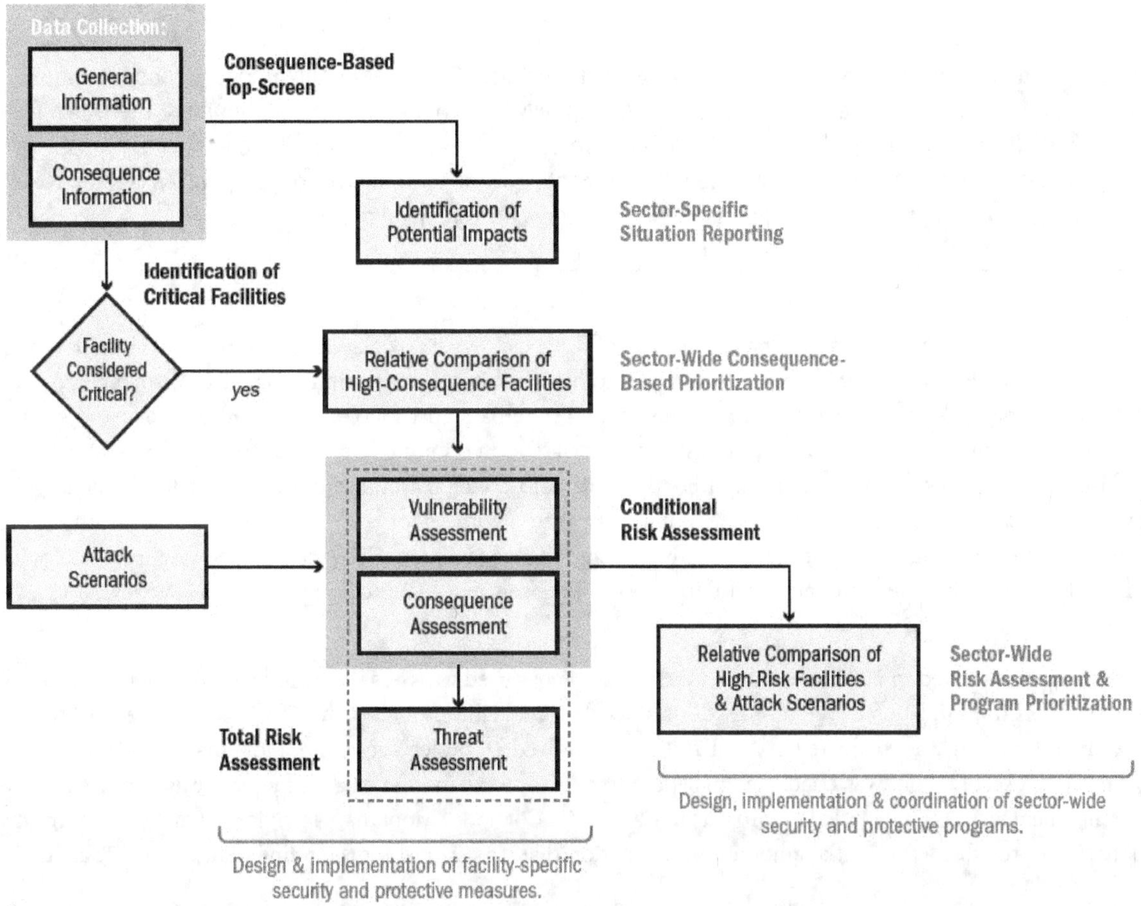

The conditional risk assessment methodology developed for sector-wide assessment would use only some of the information associated with the facility-specific assessments voluntarily offered by owners and operators. It is important to highlight that this approach does not need information from all sector assets because only a relatively small set would have significant contributions to the sector's overall risk. It is clear that some private owners may have some concerns about the voluntary submittal of this information, mainly based on the ability to protect shared information.

Finally, DHS will be responsible for conducting and facilitating the national cross-sector risk assessment. Because this analysis will be based on the results from sector-wide assessments, current efforts are focused on the development of consistent metrics to quantify the relevant risk variables.

Achieving optimal interoperability of risk assessment methods at different levels and the compatibility of risk results requires synchronization of multiple requirements. For example, facility-specific assessment methodologies must meet the needs of owners and operators who use them to secure their assets and develop facility-specific emergency action, security, response, and recovery plans. Sector-wide risk assessments must have the ability to compare, consolidate, and prioritize basic results and information from facility-specific analyses. Finally, sector-specific assessments must also provide data that is deemed reasonably compatible with assessment results from the 18 CIKR sectors to facilitate DHS national-level analysis.

3.2 Screening Infrastructure

The CTS methodology was developed to identify and characterize the subset of high-consequence facilities within the sector whose failure or disruption could potentially lead to the most severe impacts. The Dams Sector established a joint Top-Screen Workgroup to oversee the development of this screening approach. This workgroup, made up of experts from private industry, State governments, and Federal agencies, served a key role in the development and implementation of this sector-wide screening methodology.

Identifying the sector's critical assets is the first component of the sector-wide risk assessment framework. Decision making and budget allocation at the Federal and State levels with regard to national and regional infrastructure assessment, prioritization, and response coordination efforts demand a comprehensive and systematic methodology to identify critical assets. Since only a relatively small percentage of those thousands of assets may be associated with potential consequences of sector-level significance, a consequence-based screening tool is required to identify those which are most critical. Considering the large number of assets within the sector, the Dams SSA has successfully collaborated with sector partners to develop a screening approach that can effectively identify and characterize the subset of high-consequence facilities. This type of screening methodology is scalable and it could be effectively implemented at different portfolio levels (e.g., national, regional, and State levels) by adopting the appropriate consequence thresholds.

The methodology was piloted in 2008 as a way to validate the ranges used to assess the different consequence parameters, as well as to support the validation of the thresholds used to identify facilities potentially associated with sector-level consequences. A first pilot effort was conducted in April 2008 that involved 26 projects in Idaho, Montana, Nevada, Oregon, and Washington State. A second pilot was conducted in September 2008 to expand the data set by including additional projects with different characteristics; it included 22 projects in California, Colorado, Montana, New Jersey, Ohio, and Pennsylvania. These pilot efforts provided a substantial amount of information that was critical for the refinement of the CTS methodology.

Information collected through the CTS methodology is used to identify high-consequence facilities within the Dams Sector. In addition, conducting a screening of high-consequence projects provides a great opportunity to consolidate other data that may be extremely relevant in providing a full description of the relative importance of a given project and its primary functions. Furthermore, as indicated in Figure 3-4, the information collected through this effort will be valuable in supporting the overall situational awareness picture that is critically necessary for DHS to effectively conduct sector-specific reporting during incidents related to natural hazards or manmade events.

A worst reasonable case scenario must be assumed for implementation of the screening approach. This scenario considers total or extremely severe damage or disruption to the facility, without simultaneous occurrence of multiple independent extreme events or human error. The worst reasonable case scenario must provide a practical upper bound for the total potential impacts associated with severe damage or disruption, regardless of the triggering event.

Defining a reasonable scenario for consequence assessment requires determining an appropriate pool elevation. The objective is to establish the appropriate hydraulic condition that can be reasonably assumed at the site. In spite of the fact that this consequence assessment is conducted without any specific reference to a particular threat or hazard, it must be assumed that the severe damage or disruption will take place under the worst reasonable conditions at the site and a conservative pool elevation must be selected to represent an upper bound for the normal operating range. The pool elevation corresponding to the "top of active storage" provides, in most cases, a convenient condition for all-hazards screening. The active storage is the volume of the reservoir that is available for some use such as power generation, irrigation, flood control, water supply, and so forth. The active storage does not include flood surcharge, which is the storage volume between the top of the active storage and the maximum design pool elevation. For dams with uncontrolled spillways, the top of active storage elevation would typically correspond to the spillway crest. For dams with controlled or gated spillways, this elevation would typically correspond to an elevation at or near the top of the spillway gates. However, it must be highlighted that for some projects with unique characteristics, an alternate pool elevation may be more appropriate for this type of all-hazards consequence analysis. Careful engineering judgment must be used in establishing alternate pool elevations for consequence estimation.

It is important to note that the methodology does not consider the structural condition or vulnerability of the facility nor does it address the likelihood of the triggering natural hazard or manmade incident. The CTS methodology is implemented through a questionnaire that can be completed by the appropriate stakeholder using a Web-based, password-protected portal. The CTS questionnaire includes a number of tables that allow users to select, from pre-established ranges, the appropriate values that are applicable to the facility. The 14 consequence parameters that constitute the core of the screening methodology are detailed in Table 2-4. It must be noted that some of the parameters provide only a measure of project "capacity" and not necessarily a measure of direct consequences. However, it is assumed that they indirectly provide a convenient representation of the total consequences associated with failure or disruption.

A set of thresholds is defined for some of the consequence parameters to identify those facilities that are considered critical within the sector (i.e., those high-consequence facilities whose failure or disruption could be potentially associated with the highest possible impacts compared to other sector assets). A facility that reaches any of these conditions is considered part of the sector list of critical assets. This type of screening is certainly scalable and can be conducted not only at the sector level, but also at the State or regional level by defining the appropriate values for the thresholds corresponding to the different consequence parameters.

The CTS methodology for dams was initially implemented during 2009 and its results will be updated annually. A CTS methodology for levees is under development and will capitalize on the inventory and screening efforts under the USACE and FEMA levee safety initiatives.

3.3 Assessing Consequences

Methodologies to characterize the consequences associated with critical assets will be developed, as necessary, in collaboration with sector partners through their voluntary participation. A main objective is to develop a consistent definition of consequences because it is one of the important variables affecting risk.

As defined in the NIPP, consequences can be divided into four main categories:

- **Public Health and Safety:** The effects on human life and physical well-being (e.g., fatalities, injuries/illness, etc.).

- **Economic:** Direct and indirect economic losses (e.g., the cost to rebuild the asset, the cost to respond to and recover from an attack or incident, the downstream costs resulting from disruption of a product or service, and long-term costs due to environmental damage).

- **Psychological:** The effects on public morale and confidence in national economic and political institutions (encompassing changes in perception emerging after a significant incident that affects the public's sense of safety and well-being and can manifest in aberrant behavior).

- **Government/Mission Impact:** The effects on government's or industry's ability to maintain order, deliver minimum essential public services, ensure public health and safety, and carry out national security-related missions.

An assessment of consequences in all of these categories may be beyond the capabilities and resources typically available to sector asset owners. At a minimum, consequence assessments should focus on the two most fundamental impacts: public health and safety and the most relevant direct economic impacts.

A cyber attack may also produce significant consequences. Although attacks on a cyber system may involve only the cyber components and their operation, their impact can extend into the physical, business, human, and environmental systems to which they are connected. A cyber event, whether caused by an external adversary, an insider threat, or inadequate policies and procedures, can initiate a loss of system control, resulting in negative consequences. As described in Section 1.1.3, a successful cyber attack could have significant public health and safety impacts, as well as economic impacts.

The best method for assessing the consequences of a full or partial dam failure is traditional dam-break studies that have been used by the industry for years. These models allow the identification of the downstream population and property that would be affected by the failure. The dam industry in the United States has accumulated volumes of information related to the specific consequences arising from emergencies at major U.S. dams as a result of more than 30 years of dam safety experience and activities. However, in some cases, these simulations have been carried out using one-dimensional models that cannot fully capture the dynamics of highly dynamic floods resulting from the failure of dams.

Undoubtedly, one-dimensional models for dam-break inundation analysis have several attractive features. Experience has shown that, when appropriately used, these models can provide reliable results even under relatively complex conditions. The corresponding numerical simulations generally run faster; however, the preparation of the cross-section data may take considerable time and, in some cases, engineering judgment may be required to select the location of the cross-sections and their width. The considerable amount of experience accumulated in the dam engineering community regarding one-dimensional models is also a very important factor. However, in practice, one encounters many situations where one-dimensional models are not appropriate. Errors may arise when the dam is very high and the initial water difference between upstream and downstream is large. Many of the one-dimensional, unsteady flow models currently being used cannot handle the mixed-flow regimes that can be present in highly dynamic dam-break floods. Sudden changes in cross-section may constitute a serious challenge for these models, which assume that the flow reaching a cross-section takes up as much width as it can. Therefore, these models cannot provide sufficiently accurate results when the flow is not channelized or the dam-break flood propagates on a flat terrain.

The most common objections against the use of two-dimensional models are the long computational times and the detailed input data needed. However, recent scientific and technological developments have made these models much more accessible and practical. Considerable advances in geographic information systems and remote-sensing technologies have facilitated data preparation for advanced two-dimensional models. Digital elevation maps and remote-sensing images can be used efficiently to set up more realistic simulations of dam failure scenarios involving the use of two-dimensional models or coupled one- and two-dimensional models.

Once the extent of the inundation corresponding to the selected scenario has been determined, the impacts on public health and safety can be obtained through determination of the associated population at risk and the potential loss of life. Several approaches are currently available for estimating the loss of life resulting from dam failure. Some of the most well-known models are those developed by the Bureau of Reclamation, Utah State University, and BC Hydro. Each loss-of-life estimation method attempts to determine if people will be located in an unsafe situation when the dam failure floodwaters arrive. Each methodology, either directly or indirectly, uses estimates or assumptions regarding the issuance of warnings, people's responses to warnings, and the flood lethality for people exposed to the flood. Loss of life is likely if, due to a lack of warning or a failure to respond to a warning, people are exposed to rapidly rising, deep, and swiftly moving water and are not in a structure that can withstand the flooding.

The economic losses arising from a dam or levee failure, however, are much more difficult to determine. If an emergency were to occur, such as a complete or partial dam or levee failure, infrastructure located downstream of the dam or proximate to a levee could be affected based on the specific flood hydraulics involved in the failure scenario. A dam or levee located upstream of other dams or levees could potentially cause one or more downstream dams or levees to fail in a cascading manner, thus significantly increasing the overall consequences. In addition, lifelines and other industries located within the inundation area also could be adversely affected.

Addressing the downstream damages estimation problem can be effectively done by taking advantage of software products such as the risk assessment methodology HAZUS-MH (Hazards U.S.–Multi-Hazard), developed by FEMA under contract with the National Institute of Building Sciences. HAZUS-MH is a nationally applicable standardized methodology and risk assessment software program for analyzing potential losses from floods, hurricane winds, and earthquakes. In particular, HAZUS-MH includes a number of depth-damage functions that relate water depth to structure and content percent damage, which, in turn, provides the ability to determine the damages resulting from a dam failure based on flood depth and extent.

There are significant dependencies and interdependencies within the Dams Sector and among the Dams Sector and other sectors, especially Water, Energy, and Transportation. As a result, the risk assessment of an individual dam or levee system should take into account the potential for impacts to and from other infrastructure sectors and cascading consequences. Having the ability to quantify dependencies and interdependencies with a high level of certainty will continue to be a challenge for many asset owners. Some progress has been made in quantifying some of these interdependencies, but more work and developed methodologies are needed.

The Dams Sector also includes assets potentially associated with adverse consequences that could affect international interdependencies. For example, several dams are located along our common borders with Canada and Mexico. Those dams should be evaluated for risk and subsequent consequences to determine if they would have any significant adverse effect on the involved countries.

Consequences in the Dams Sector are assumed to be dynamic, given the nature of the potential population growth downstream, so they must be evaluated continually and factored into the sector's overall assessment of risk. Alterations in the consequence assessment could derive from increased urbanization and economic development in the downstream reaches of a dam or the inundation area of a levee. The consequences will also change based on seasonal or periodic variations in reservoir and water levels.

In some cases, the quantification of consequences needs to take into account that assets may constitute a system closely interconnected by function or spatial location. A system of multiple assets (SMA) is defined as a set of individual or structurally independent facilities that are not necessarily located in spatial proximity of each other or within a single project, but that work together to perform one or more primary functions. For example, an integrated flood damage reduction system may include a number of structures and components (e.g., spillways, pump stations, etc.) that are essential to the function of the system, but are not located within the same local area. Depending on the common primary functions that they jointly support, the assets could be spatially distributed across the same watershed or within the same floodplain. In this case, the loss, failure, or disruption of any of the individual facilities constituting the SMA may trigger consequences affecting the ability of the entire system to meet its critical function. Therefore, consequence estimates for these types of closely interconnected facilities must reflect any corresponding system-wide effects.

As noted earlier, a consistent definition of consequences is one of the important variables affecting risk assessments. Sector-wide guidelines for consistent approaches to estimating the public health and economic impacts resulting from dam or levee failure, regardless of the triggering event, must be built into the risk assessment framework to ensure consistency across the sector. Several sector partners, including the Dams SSA and the Bureau of Reclamation, are actively collaborating on the development of guidelines for consistent estimation of loss of life and economic consequences resulting from dam failure. The proposed consequence estimation guidelines consider direct economic losses from downstream damages to property and infrastructure, losses in project benefits (e.g., loss of agricultural irrigation, municipal and industrial water services, and power generation), reconstruction and/or repair costs, and indirect impacts on the affected regional economy. Recognizing that the proposed economic assessment methodology is very data and resource intensive, an alternate estimation methodology based on PAR is under consideration. In this alternate methodology, an estimate of the expected direct damages is determined as a function of the corresponding PAR. This approach could be applicable for an economic impact estimation analysis of smaller facilities and could also support expedited portfolio screening efforts across the sector.

3.4 Assessing Vulnerabilities

Vulnerability assessments identify the physical features or operational attributes that could render an entity open to exploitation or susceptible to a given hazard. Vulnerabilities vary from project to project and could be related to deficiencies in construction, access control, operations, maintenance, or security systems. Risk assessments conducted to date that incorporate vulnerability assessment components have been made primarily at the facility-specific level.

Federal agency members of the Dams Sector are very proactive in developing vulnerability assessment methods and are consistently evaluating and suggesting enhancements to existing methodologies to meet current and future needs. Non-Federal dam owners subject to FERC jurisdiction follow FERC and industry-developed security guidance and conduct vulnerability assessments of those facilities potentially associated with the most significant impacts.

Because of the wide variation in asset characteristics within the Dams Sector, CIKR partners use a wide range of security vulnerability assessment methodologies that may differ in terms of overall approach, comprehensiveness, duration of study, and resource and expertise requirements. No single methodology has been adopted to date or is being promoted across the sector for use at the facility-specific level. In fact, throughout this section, the term "vulnerability assessment" is used to represent a process, not a specific vulnerability assessment methodology. Each owner and operator within the Dams Sector must decide, on a self-assessment basis, the aspects to consider and the appropriate depth of vulnerability analysis required for individual facilities. This complicates the comparison of vulnerability assessment results across the sector.

Appendix 5 provides additional information on asset-specific vulnerability assessments, describing the most important elements to be included in assessments conducted at the facility level and providing a summary of the vulnerability assessment tools commonly used across the Dams Sector, particularly by those entities involved in power generation.

The common elements of a vulnerability assessment are as follows:

• Identifying the vulnerabilities associated with physical, cyber, or human factors; crucial dependencies; and hazard scenarios;

• Describing all protective measures in place and how they reduce the vulnerability for each scenario; and

• Developing estimates of the likelihood of success associated with each scenario.

If the vulnerability, V, is defined probabilistically, then it represents the probability that a given type of attack against an asset will be successful, if attempted. Any vulnerability quantified in this manner conforms to the mathematical rules governing probabilities and its value (ranging from zero to one) can be combined multiplicatively with the value of the consequences, C. For a given attack scenario, this product of V and C produces a consistent metric of conditional risk (Rc). As mentioned before, a sector-wide conditional risk evaluation could offer extremely useful insight on the attack types that could affect large segments of the sector or its subsectors. It is important to highlight that determination of sector-wide conditional risk would require an estimation of the vulnerability (i.e., the probability of success given an attack) only for those critical facilities that would contribute the most to the overall risk picture.

Estimates of probabilities clearly benefit from having historical and experiential data as a basis for estimation and this is not readily available in the case of successful terrorist attacks. However, the absence of data does not preclude estimating probability. In data-poor environments, experts using experience, modeling, and other tools of inference can estimate probability, which is commonly referred to as "subjective probability."

An ideal methodology would need to include a rigorous and repeatable procedure for estimating the probability of success given an attack, assuming that an attack was attempted in the first place. A straightforward way of doing this would be to systematically elicit this information from a panel of sector security experts based on the attack scenario, generic characteristics of representative assets, and the type of security measures in place. This probability would not be calculated each time for each asset; however, once determined and systematically validated, it would be made readily accessible in a series of tables listing the probabilities of success versus generic security configurations for general facility types. The resulting vulnerability estimation process could be consistently applied for sector-wide analysis. It must be noted that the scope of this approach is limited to sector-wide comparative analysis and does not replace or duplicate detailed facility-specific vulnerability assessments.

Common and emerging sector vulnerabilities will be assessed continuously through periodic discussions among the SSA and the sector councils, including classified discussions when necessary. Vulnerabilities will also be identified through the reporting of incidents and through R&D capability gap identification efforts.

3.5 Assessing Threats

The remaining factor to be considered in the risk assessment process is the analysis, evaluation, and quantification of the threat variable. Calculating the threat posed by adversaries is one of the most pressing challenges in the risk management community. Although local information is generally readily available for facility-level threat analysis, sector-level threat data remains historically sparse. Intelligence reporting is a main source of adversary threat data, but it is often incomplete and sometimes conflicting. Analytical products are generally not written with the premise that their output will be directly quantified or will result in explicit probabilistic estimations, which complicates the direct incorporation of threat data into risk assessments.

In the context of terrorist risk assessment, the threat variable needs to be expressed as the likelihood of a terrorist attack method on a particular facility or type of facility. The estimate of this likelihood is based on an analysis of the intent and capability of a defined adversary, taking into consideration historical activities (domestic and overseas) and taking into account the corresponding operational environment. How might an ideal methodology assign a probability, over a given time period, for an attack on a given type of asset? Well-established methods of expert elicitation could be effectively used to process the available intelligence information and systematically generate numerical estimates for different potential threats. The estimates should be derived through a collaborative process involving the intelligence and risk analysis communities. The probability could be derived by first assigning a value to the probability of a significant attack on U.S. critical infrastructure and then multiplying this value by the likelihood that, given an attack, it would be aimed at the sector being considered (in this case, the Dams Sector). Finally, one would have to assign a probability that the attack on this sector would be conducted against a specific type of dam or a particular dam. Extensions of the technique would include various probabilities estimated for different types of significant attack scenarios. The set of plausible attack scenarios should be determined through active collaboration among intelligence and risk analysts. This process is fundamentally different from those cases involving natural disasters or accidents, for which the likelihood estimate is typically based on a probability of occurrence that relies on historical data and the physical characteristics of the system.

3.5.1 Sources of Threat Information

Information about terrorism or criminal threats against the sector originates from a number of sources, including the following:

- Reports by owners and operators of threats, actual incidents, or suspicious activities (e.g., elicitation, overflights, surveillance, etc.);

- Intelligence information and related criminal investigations by Federal, State, and local law enforcement agencies;

- Intelligence information regarding terrorist intentions by the various national intelligence services; and

- DHS sector-specific analysis of potential threats against the Dams Sector.

Several sources of intelligence information are available to the Dams Sector. A primary source is the DHS Homeland Infrastructure Threat and Risk Analysis Center (HITRAC), which conducts integrated threat and risk analyses for all CIKR sectors. HITRAC is a joint program office that incorporates capabilities and resources from the DHS Office of Intelligence and Analysis—a member of the intelligence community—and the DHS Office of Infrastructure Protection. HITRAC brings together intelligence and infrastructure specialists to ensure a sufficient understanding of the risks to the Nation's infrastructure from foreign and domestic threats. HITRAC works in partnership with the U.S. intelligence community and national law enforcement to effectively integrate and analyze intelligence and law enforcement information in threat and risk analyses products. In addition, USACE and the Bureau of Reclamation host intelligence centers that serve their infrastructure. FERC participates in the USACE real-time database on threats and suspicious incidents and shares pertinent information with the owners and operators of dams under its jurisdiction, as appropriate. In return, dam owners regulated by FERC provide threat data to the database. Each Federal Bureau of Investigation (FBI) field headquarters has a Joint Terrorism Task Force that is generally available as a resource to non-Federal dam owners to assist them in identifying potential threats to their facilities. The FBI Threat Review Unit reviews and attempts to resolve suspicious activities and threats reported to the bureau.

Uniformity in reporting criteria aids efficient communication of threats and is achieved by developing universally accepted reporting criteria and providing access to the appropriate information repositories. The Dams Sector Information Sharing Workgroup collaborated with the Dams SSA in the implementation of effective mechanisms for notification of urgent alerts and warnings using the Executive Notification Service, managed by the National Infrastructure Coordinating Center (NICC). The NICC is a DHS watch operations center that maintains operational awareness of the Nation's CIKR and provides mechanisms and tools for sharing critical information among government and industry partners in response to CIKR-related incidents.

In addition, the Dams Sector implemented a Suspicious Activity Report online tool within the Homeland Security Information Network–Critical Sectors (HSIN-CS) Dams Portal to provide users with the capability to report and retrieve information pertaining to suspicious activities that may potentially be associated with pre-incident surveillance, activities exploring or targeting a critical infrastructure facility or system, or any possible violation of law or regulation that could compromise the facility or system in a manner that could cause an incident jeopardizing life or property. The online tool does not replace existing agency or organizational reporting mechanisms but instead enhances them by providing a broader, horizontal approach to reporting suspicious activities. While suspicious activities should always be reported to the appropriate authorities, this online tool is utilized to provide an extra opportunity for real-time situational awareness across the sector.

To ensure that threats against the Dams Sector on a national level are better understood, the SSA, GCC, and SCC work together to evaluate and understand threat information with regard to the sector as a whole. This interaction includes ongoing dialogue with HITRAC and other DHS components through periodic sector meetings to discuss specific, generic, and potential threats directed against the industry. Consistent with achieving the sector's goal of increasing communication and building partnerships, many CIKR partners have obtained the necessary security clearances to allow them to participate in classified briefings and discussions.

The Dams Sector also develops unclassified communications that can be distributed more broadly through existing communication channels, such as the notification systems of the National Hydropower Association, USSD, the National Mining Association, ASDSO, and FERC. In addition, hydropower generation facilities have the capability to tie into the Electric Sector Information Sharing and Analysis Center (ISAC), which issues regular threat alerts regarding computer systems and cybersecurity.

Individual asset owners and operators are encouraged to establish strong relationships with the local law enforcement agencies that have jurisdiction over their facilities, as well as local FBI field offices. DHS Protective Security Advisors (PSAs) also provide assistance and coordination at the local level and they can be an effective resource for owners and operators.

3.5.2 Sector Threat Environment

The general threat environment for the Dams Sector is highly variable. Historically, threat activities against dams in the United States have been limited to demonstrations, vandalism, and minor criminal activities. Incidents involving U.S. dams have been on a small scale, but past plots by violent domestic extremists and previous interest in U.S. dams by transnational terrorist groups indicate a need for continued vigilance and prompt reporting of suspicious activities by security personnel and dam owners. The magnitude of the potential consequences of a dam failure, particularly of those near large population centers, constitutes an important element in the sector risk profile. In addition, the sector's dependency on digital communications and the convergence of control systems with public and private business networks have also high-

Responding as the Threat Level Increases

The steady-state security posture of a facility may change as threat levels escalate. For example, a facility may modify its visitor access procedures as follows:

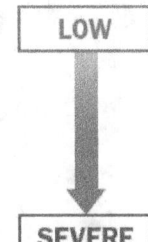

LOW → SEVERE

- Use passive security measures to keep the public at safe distances from critical project assets for their safety.
- Limit public access to non-critical project assets only.
- Require all public visitors to non-critical assets to wear identification badges and be escorted.
- Discontinue public visits.
- Request that local authorities close public roads to and near the project.

lighted the possibility of cyber threats, which may range from theft of business data to intrusions into critical control systems and disruption of system operations.

Real-time analysis of emergent threats or immediate incidents is of great value to CIKR partners and helps them determine if changes are needed in their steady-state security posture. If any specific threat information is available through intelligence sources, that information will be distributed to CIKR partners to drive short-term protective measures and contribute to their understanding of the sector's dynamic threat environment. In some cases, however, short-term protective measures for specific threats may not be possible, reasonable, or prudent because of the required engineering lead times and construction procurements. In addition, determining appropriate and effective protective measures depends a great deal on site- and threat-specific conditions. Thus, the protective response focuses on the inherent vulnerabilities of different assets and the potential consequences if the assets were attacked, rather than on the likelihood of a particular event.

4. Prioritize Infrastructure

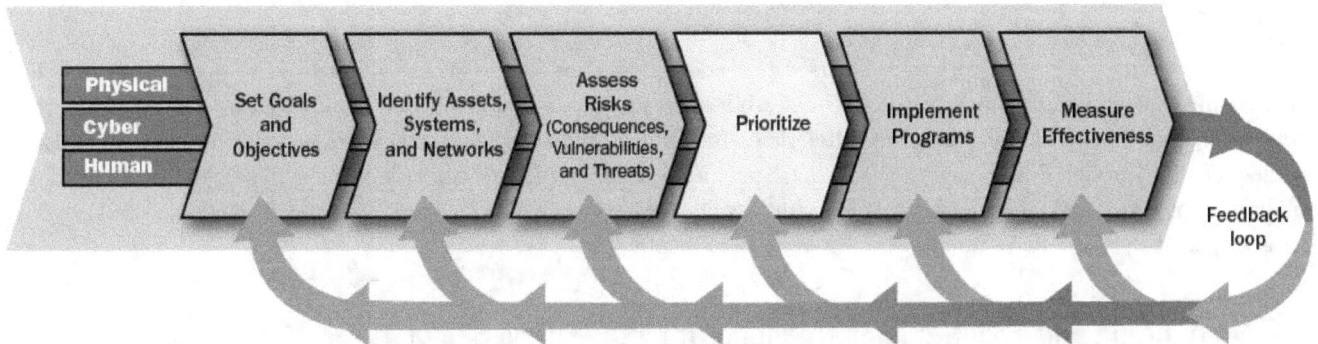

Continuous improvement to enhance protection of CIKR

The Nation's infrastructure and associated protective programs must be prioritized on the basis of risk to ensure that resources are applied in areas that will most enhance the mitigation of risk. Systematic methods for prioritizing sector assets, as well as any corresponding protective actions, offer transparency and increase the defensibility of resource allocation decisions.

This chapter focuses on a risk-based process intended to facilitate a systematic prioritization of the critical assets within the Dams Sector. This process will also provide the basis for the corresponding prioritization of sector-wide protection programs and resilience-enhancing strategies.

As described in chapter 3, there are three general risk assessment levels: (1) facility-specific, (2) sector-wide, and (3) cross-sector. Each risk assessment level can support the corresponding prioritization efforts. For example, facility-specific analysis can support prioritization efforts conducted by an owner or operator on the corresponding internal portfolio. Due to the limitations and lack of interoperability of asset-level methodologies, these results cannot easily support comparisons with other methodologies used by other owners or regulatory agencies. On the other hand, sector-wide risk assessment can support a much broader prioritization scope, which includes those facilities that are most critical within the sector. The cross-sector analysis is performed by DHS as part of the national comparative risk assessment effort, with the goal of establishing priorities across multiple sectors.

The prioritization process involves aggregating, combining, and analyzing risk assessment results to determine which assets face the highest risk. This process leads to a comprehensive picture of risk for the relevant CIKR groups and allows protection priorities to be established; it also provides the basis for understanding the risk mitigation benefits that, along with costs, are used to support protection planning and the informed allocation of resources.

The Dams Sector will implement a systematic identification and prioritization of those assets associated with high-risk conditions. The overall process must follow a series of logical steps to narrow down the universe of sector assets to those with potentially significant consequences at a national level (critical assets) and then identify which ones are at high-risk conditions (the most critical assets). The process will be a combined, continuous effort of the SSA and its public and private sector partners.

As mentioned in chapter 3, the Dams SSA and GCC and SCC members worked collaboratively to develop the CTS methodology to screen assets based on their consequences. The SSA will continue to work with all sector partners and request their input to update, refine, or develop consequence and vulnerability assessment methodologies that can be useful in supporting the sector-wide, risk-based prioritization of critical assets.

Considering the breadth of sources that contribute to asset lists, as well as the number of facility-specific assessment methodologies available within the Dams Sector (see Appendix 5), it will be very important to integrate the results from existing vulnerability studies successfully into a sector-wide methodology that produces a consistent risk assessment for the Dams Sector. The sector-wide risk assessment framework displayed in Figure 3-4 may provide an effective tool to accomplish this. However, as noted above, information safeguarding concerns still remain significant enough that its voluntary sector-wide adoption is not yet ensured.

The Dams SSA will continue to work with all applicable Federal, State, and local agencies with dam security responsibilities to improve the current understanding of existing vulnerability assessment methodologies and work with asset owners to integrate information from the results obtained using different methodologies into a single and consistent sector-wide conditional risk framework. It is through this leveraging of data that a practical evaluation of the sector risk profile will be generated, avoiding duplication of efforts and taking advantage of existing results. Automation would facilitate faster report generation and provide the ability to analyze and make comparisons between assessments.

4.1 Normalizing and Prioritizing Information Within the Dams Sector

Since the Dams Sector is currently using many different methodologies to assess vulnerabilities and consequences, a mechanism must be developed to accommodate the information generated by those methodologies into a sector-wide scheme for risk-based prioritization of sector critical assets.

4.1.1 Normalization of Risk Variables

Risk assessment methodologies currently in use across the Dams Sector are based on different assumptions and approaches, yielding solutions that cannot be easily compared. These methodologies are extremely useful for facility-specific assessments, but their output cannot be directly used to support sector-level analysis. A sector-wide prioritization must be based on risk assessment results that support an objective comparison across the sector. A conditional risk approach (based on consequences and vulnerabilities for generic attack vectors) provides a simple and defensible framework for sector-wide prioritization purposes.

This sector-wide approach can make use of the information generated via facility-specific assessments by introducing a suitable normalization process. This will provide a consistent framework that will allow, for example, the development of consistent estimates of vulnerabilities for each critical facility based on information already available. This is a great advantage as there is no need for a complicated security analysis for each facility under consideration or a detailed model to estimate the probability of success of a given attack against a given target.

At a minimum, detailed consequence and vulnerability facility-level assessments should be completed for all sector critical assets by their owners and operators. This asset-specific assessment should be redone when security upgrades have been completed to validate the claimed level of risk reduction. Additional risk assessments should be made on a regular and periodic basis, or when conditions change, such as when threat levels or substantial changes to the facility or downstream infrastructure occur. These asset-specific assessments, as conducted by the owners, will provide the results that are needed to implement the sector-wide assessment.

Dams Sector GCC and SCC members are collaborating to determine the data reporting requirements for characterizing sector assets. Currently, the Bureau of Reclamation, USACE, and TVA have made significant progress in completing, retaining, and initiating the recommendations of many risk and vulnerability assessments. Private and State-regulated hydroelectric utilities under FERC jurisdiction also have completed the required assessments of vulnerability and risk at their most significant facilities. However, many owners of municipal dams have not completed consequence assessments or vulnerability studies. The number of unregulated private sector dams that have actually completed vulnerability studies is unknown at this time and represents a data gap that the Dams Sector needs to address in the future. Enactment of the recommendation of the National Committee on Levee Safety to expand the National Levee Database to include a one-time USACE inventory and inspection of all non-Federal levees would lead to a greater understanding of critical levees and their potential contribution to the overall risk profile of the sector.

4.1.2 Sector-Wide Prioritization

Conducting a risk-based prioritization of assets requires a clear and consistent screening strategy. Considering the large number of assets in the sector, it is necessary to determine the subset of facilities potentially associated with the most severe consequences. These critical facilities constitute the candidate assets for inclusion in the sector-wide conditional risk assessment.

After conducting the corresponding risk assessment, the set of critical assets can be prioritized consistently; those sector assets at highest risk for each one of the different attack vectors considered would constitute the most critical assets for the sector. Figure 4-2 presents this process.

Figure 4-2: Sector-Specific Prioritization of Assets

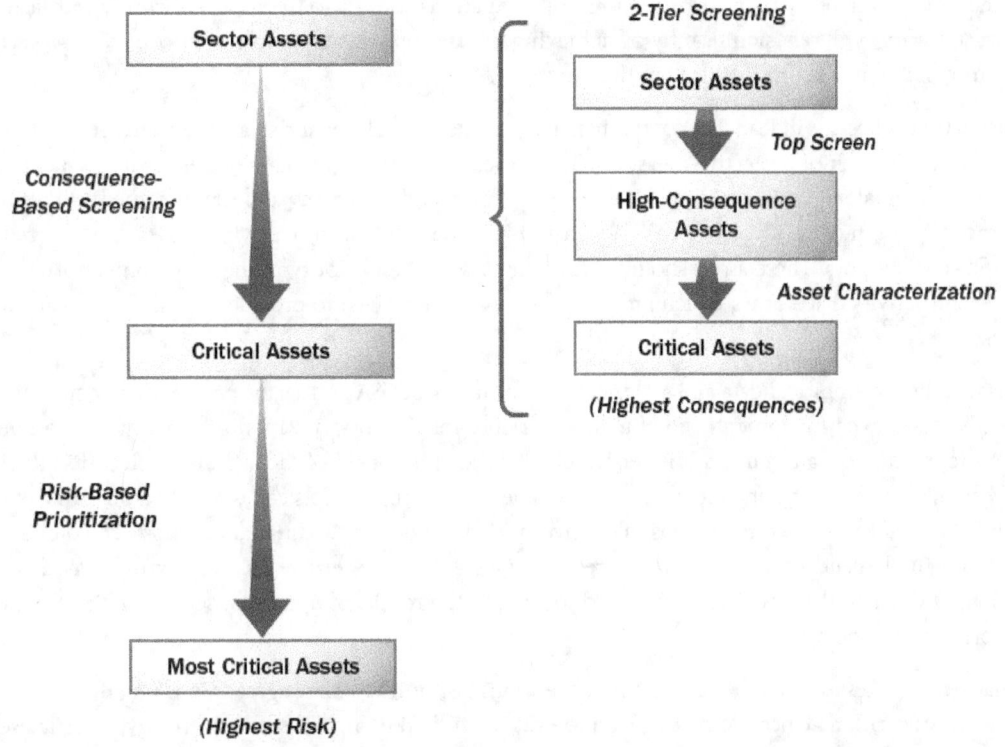

Therefore, from a practical implementation standpoint, an accurate and consistent consequence-based screening, such as that done through the CTS, is essential to achieve a meaningful prioritization, because it provides the starting set of facilities. A key element of this process is the definition of the sector criticality criteria used in the CTS approach. These sector criticality thresholds allow the consistent identification of those facilities that could be associated with the most significant consequences.

Furthermore, there are recognized differences among national critical assets, sector critical assets, State critical assets, and owner-identified critical assets. Asset criticality depends on the particular definitions or numerical thresholds used, since it is a relative concept. Therefore, asset criticality has to be defined with respect to a given scale. DHS, in collaboration with the SSAs and State governments, is responsible for leading the cross-sector effort that defines the critical assets at the national level. Assets held by private companies have critical missions germane to the company's continuity of operations, economic health, and viability; however, State and national officials may not recognize or understand the criticality of these facilities. The SCC is charged with developing an awareness strategy for the critical nature of private facilities.

At this time, no current or reliable estimates can be provided for the total number of critical assets within the Dams Sector, but it is expected that multiple iterations of the CTS annual process will converge to achieve a finite number of facilities. Alterations in the definitions of the criticality criteria used in the CTS could change the number and distribution of dams in the preliminary screening and subsequent prioritization. Gaps still exist in identifying sector assets (significant gaps exist for levees) and it is expected that a continually improving process will be needed to resolve this issue. It is anticipated that, in the future, all relevant information associated with the sector's critical assets will be housed within the Infrastructure Data Warehouse domain, assuming that the appropriate data-protection mechanisms are in place.

Using the list of critical assets derived from CTS implementation, the SSA will collaborate with sector partners to conduct a risk-based prioritization of these critical assets using a conditional risk approach. The specific dams or levees with the highest potential for consequences will be encouraged to complete a voluntary and detailed risk assessment made on a self-assessment basis. Many owners of less critical assets may realize the benefits of conducting such assessments and also may choose to complete assessments on a voluntary basis, or as required by regulations specific to them. As previously indicated, the successful completion of this effort will rely significantly on achieving the appropriate assurances of information protection, thereby facilitating the participation of the private sector in the process.

The sector prioritization process will lead to a comprehensive picture of conditional risk for the Dams Sector and will allow the corresponding prioritization of protective measures. This process will also provide the basis for understanding the risk mitigation benefits, which, along with costs, are used to support protection planning and the informed allocation of resources. Therefore, the prioritization process involves two related activities. The first determines which assets are exposed to the greatest risk for specific attack vectors. These assets should be assigned the highest priority in the development of risk management programs. The second activity determines which protective actions are expected to provide the most practical and cost-effective mitigation of risk.

Even with the availability of empirical data and systematic procedures, the SSA and sector partners will continue to factor subject matter knowledge, expert judgment, and human experience into the prioritization process, which will help shape the recommendations to executive management. It is very likely that most, if not all, of the facilities included in the list of critical assets already have completed vulnerability and risk assessments. Existing models can calculate a relative risk score for an asset's security posture and account for reductions in relative risk on the basis of additional or enhanced countermeasures. As an owner or operator implements new security measures for a given asset, the relative risk score will be recalculated to reflect a new risk condition. Owners of assets will be encouraged to provide the results of updated asset-specific risk assessments voluntarily for the prioritization process.

A maximum relative risk threshold will be suggested for the Dams Sector if it can be agreed on mutually. The data required to substantiate the relative risk may need to be collected to evaluate fully the implied security effectiveness. Those assets that exceed the maximum relative risk threshold may be encouraged to implement additional security countermeasures to reduce the risk of high-consequence threat scenarios. Owners of those assets will be encouraged to implement additional countermeasures to reduce their risk scores.

The proposed development of a methodology to facilitate the sector-wide and cross-sector comparison of risk variables is expected to provide an alternative mechanism to convert and compare the results obtained with different assessment methodologies. Implementation of this tool could take advantage of the information already available; it also could provide a straightforward standard approach for sector prioritization of critical assets.

To validate the level of risk reduction realized when upgrades to security have been made at specific sites, it may be appropriate to reassess and, if necessary, modify the sector prioritization. Additional adjustments to the prioritized list should also be made if conditions change, such as changes in the threat level or substantial changes to the facility or downstream infrastructure.

5. Develop and Implement Protective Programs and Resilience Strategies

Figure 5-1: Implementing Sector Protective Programs

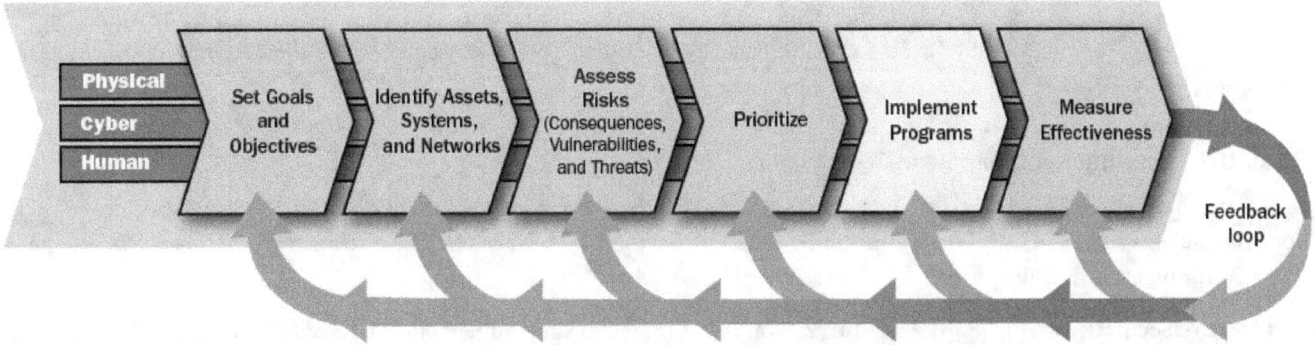

Continuous improvement to enhance protection of CIKR

Effective protective programs and resilience strategies for the Dams Sector must be risk-based and support the sector's vision and goals. The NIPP defines these programs and strategies as actions to mitigate the overall risk to CIKR assets, systems, networks, functions, or their interconnecting links, which can take the form of deterring threats, mitigating vulnerabilities, or minimizing the consequences of manmade or natural hazards. CIKR protection can also include improving security protocols; hardening facilities; building resilience and redundancy into design and operations; incorporating hazard resistance into facility design; initiating active or passive countermeasures; installing security systems; promoting workforce surety programs; implementing cybersecurity measures; conducting training and exercises; and developing and testing continuity, response, and emergency action plans.

This expansive definition of protective programs and resilience strategies is consistent with the range of activities used by various Dams Sector CIKR partners. Because of the large number and diversity of assets, security postures, business cases, and asset owners and operators encompassed by the Dams Sector, a "one size fits all" protective program is not appropriate. This chapter describes how CIKR partners throughout the Dams Sector develop and implement protective programs that target the physical, cyber, and human elements of sector assets. The risk management activities that stem from these programs are briefly described in chapter 6. This chapter lists examples of the types of protective and resilience measures used in the sector and describes the risk-informed, comprehensive, and cost-effective framework used by asset owners and operators in successfully developing protective programs as part of a risk management strategy. In addition, it describes the characteristics that the sector and owners and operators prefer when developing protective measures and activities to implement protective programs and resilience strategies.

5.1 Overview of Dams Sector Protective Programs and Resilience Strategies

Protective programs, resilience strategies, and specific protective measures for individual sector assets will vary greatly depending on the level of risk that encompasses the specific threat to the asset, its vulnerability, and the consequences of failure. Protective measures undertaken to upgrade security, safety, and resilience at dams include, but are not limited to, the installation of boat and vehicle barriers, enhanced access control measures, expanded CCTV coverage, increased use of alarm systems, enhanced measures to secure control systems (both physical and cyber), the integration of security into existing emergency plans, and expanded personnel screening programs. Protective measures at dams, levees, and other sector assets also include contingency planning and increased liaison with all levels of law enforcement and emergency response agencies. Nonstructural protective measures such as zoning, strengthened building codes, floodplain management ordinances, development fees, flood risk education programs, and relocation of flood-prone communities and infrastructure are examples of protective measures that can substantially decrease the impact of a levee break.

The protective framework for the Dams Sector features a variety of programs implemented at various levels. This section briefly introduces them; further descriptions are available in the 2009 Dams Sector Annual Report. This chapter concludes with a listing of the types of protective measures and resilience strategies used in the sector and a description of their coordination within the sector. Appendix 6 describes a process that some owners and operators use to develop their facility-specific protection needs.

5.1.1 U.S. Department of Homeland Security

DHS engages in protective activities, resilience strategies, initiatives, and reports that are not necessarily sector-specific, but have potential benefits across all CIKR sectors, including the Dams Sector. Examples of efforts that directly or indirectly benefit the Dams Sector include the following:

- **Protective Security Advisor (PSA) Program:** PSAs are DHS protection and vulnerability assessment specialists assigned as DHS liaisons for the Federal, State, local, tribal, and territorial governments and the private sector. PSAs are responsible for sharing risk information and providing technical assistance to local law enforcement and CIKR owners and operators within their respective areas of responsibility.

- **Buffer Zone Protection Program (BZPP):** The BZPP is a Federal grant program designed to increase the preparedness capabilities of jurisdictions responsible for the safety and security of communities surrounding high-priority CIKR assets, including chemical facilities, dams, nuclear and electric power plants, and other high-consequence facilities.

- **Training Programs:** These programs provide CIKR partners with a source from which they can obtain specialized training to enhance CIKR protection. The subject matter, course length, and location of training can be tailored to meet the partner's needs.

- **Control Systems Security Program (CSSP):** The CSSP reduces control system risks within and across all critical infrastructure sectors by coordinating efforts among Federal, State, local, and tribal governments, as well as control systems owners, operators, and vendors; reduces the likelihood of the success and the severity of impact of a cyber attack against critical infrastructure control systems through risk mitigation activities.

5.1.2 Sector-Specific Agency

The Dams SSA supports the development and implementation of protective programs and resilience strategies with a sector-wide focus. As described in Section 1.2.2, the SSA is responsible for, among other matters, coordinating, facilitating, and supporting comprehensive risk assessment and risk management strategies for high-risk CIKR; identifying protection and resilience priorities; and promoting CIKR protection education, training, and awareness within the sector.

Accordingly, the SSA coordinates Dams Sector programs to identify critical sector assets and enable quick characterization of an incident's impact at a facility or regional level. In alignment with two of the sector's goals, the SSA supports the development of reference documents on how the sector can manage risks and an R&D program to enhance sector security and resilience.

5.1.3 Owners and Operators

The owner and operator community within the Dams Sector comprises private companies; State, local, and municipal governments; agencies such as water management districts, levee boards, and utility districts; and the Federal Government. Protective program and resilience strategy elements implemented by this community depend on the criticality of the asset to the company's or agency's mission and business line, and its public health and safety consequences in the event of asset failure.

Federal CIKR owners and operators—the Bureau of Reclamation, TVA, USACE, and IBWC—are self-regulating and therefore establish their own protective programs that involve identifying their critical assets, conducting vulnerability assessments, and implementing any required recommendations.

Non-Federal owners and operators regulated by Federal and/or State agencies adhere to those agencies' requirements that are associated with protective programs. Federal and non-Federal owners and operators can also avail themselves of programs and information emanating from agencies without any specific regulatory authority over them.

5.1.4 Regulatory Agencies and Other Entities

States regulate the majority of dams in the Nation; regulation of non-Federal levees can derive from State or local government agencies. Protective programs under these agencies will vary widely; their nature and extent depend on the criticality of assets, but primarily on the agencies' statutory authorities.

FERC issues licenses to construct, operate, and maintain all project works (e.g., dams, water conduits, reservoirs, powerhouses, transmission lines, etc.) that are necessary for the development of non-Federal hydroelectric projects. FERC's safety and security regulatory structure applies to all dams under FERC's jurisdiction. In addition, FERC designated NERC as the Nation's electric reliability organization and subsequently approved the NERC-developed mandatory CIP reliability standards to protect the Nation's bulk power system against potential disruptions from cybersecurity events.

FEMA's continuing mission within DHS is to lead the effort to prepare the Nation for all hazards and to manage Federal response and recovery efforts effectively following any national incident. As the lead agency for the National Dam Safety Program, FEMA has worked for years with many sector partners on issues of national concern, including the security of dams.

FEMA is also responsible for managing the National Flood Insurance Program, which provides reduced insurance rates for persons and businesses protected by levees that have been certified as meeting FEMA requirements. Levee owners are required to provide documentation that they are in compliance with those requirements. Failure to provide that documentation can result in the decertification of the levee system and significantly higher insurance rates for those in the leveed area.

5.1.5 Cybersecurity

In addition to adherence to the NERC CIP standards, many CIKR partners develop facility- or company-specific computer incident response plans. Sector hydroelectric owners and operators use the Electric ISAC to stay informed of cyber vulnerability alerts involving enterprise software, major viruses, worms, and other cyber exploitation.

Members of the Dams SCC and GCC, as well as the SSA, also serve as members on the Cross- Sector Cybersecurity Working Group and the Industrial Control System Joint Working Group. These working groups were developed to provide further coordination on cyber-specific issues and cross-sector perspectives and knowledge regarding various cybersecurity concerns, such as common vulnerabilities and protective measures, as well as the design, development, and deployment of more secure control systems. Managing cyber risk and securing cyberspace are issues that cut across the Nation's CIKR; the cross-sector perspective helps to ensure effective coordination to address cybersecurity in a collaborative manner with all of the sectors.

Sector partners have collaborated with the Dams SSA to develop a cybersecurity roadmap that outlines an effective sector-wide framework to secure control systems. Sector stakeholders also have access to multiple control systems security guidelines and standards, such as the following:

- 21 Steps to Improve Cyber Security of SCADA Networks (DOE)
- Guide to Supervisory Control and Data Acquisition and Industrial Control Systems Security (National Institute of Standards and Technology)
- Cryptographic Protection of SCADA Communications (American Gas Association Report Number 12)
- ISA-99, Manufacturing and Control Systems Security (International Society of Automation)
- Common Cyber Security Vulnerabilities Observed in DHS Industrial Control Systems Assessments (DHS), July 2009
- Cyber Security Procurement Language for Control Systems (DHS), September 2009
- Developing an Industrial Control Systems Cybersecurity Incident Response Capability (DHS), October 2009

In addition, the DHS Control Systems Security Program conducts and facilitates multiple training courses and workshops that provide owners and operators with up-to-date information on cyber threats and mitigations for vulnerabilities.

5.1.6 Examples of Protective Measures and Resilience Strategies

Protective measures and resilience strategies put into place in the Dams Sector will vary depending on asset-specific characteristics and will consist of physical items and systems, as well as plans to address contingencies and respond to incidents. The *Dams Sector Protective Measures Handbook* provides a comprehensive list of risk reduction strategies and protective measures that could be implemented at sector assets. The following are examples of general protective measures:

Access Control

- Various levels of access control can be used depending on the critical nature of the area being accessed. Electronic entry control systems supplemented by CCTV and adequate lighting might be used for personnel entering areas of critical importance;
- Intrusion detection systems may also be activated at portals; and
- Effective locking devices may be installed at access points to gate/intake structures, galleries, vaults, and other critical locations.

Barriers

- Perimeter barriers (e.g., fences, berms, vehicle-resistant barriers, and boat barriers) could be installed to maintain a clear area at the perimeter, enable monitoring, and incorporate adequate standoff distances; and
- Intrusion barriers might be used at outlet conduits.

Monitoring and Surveillance

- CCTV cameras facilitate passive monitoring (e.g., review of a taped incident after it occurs) and active monitoring (e.g., viewing of real-time activities); and
- Detector and alarm systems (e.g., intrusion detectors, fire and smoke alarms, and motion detectors) might be integrated with surveillance systems to promote immediate assessment of any detected intrusion.

Planning and Preparedness

- Emergency action plans;
- Site security plans and threat response procedures;
- Recovery plans and continuity-of-operations plans; and
- Exercises to test the effectiveness of these plans and procedures.

Personnel

- Pre-employment criminal background checks may be conducted for new hires, seasonal employees, and temporary agency personnel; and
- Vendors, contractors, and service providers with access to critical areas and information could be required to verify that their employees have been subjected to a pre-employment criminal background check.

Communications

- Reliable communication systems (primary and alternate) may be established to provide effective channels to reach local law enforcement and emergency responders; and
- Notification protocols may be developed that outline who to contact in the event of an incident, providing staff with training and checklists.

Cyber

- Security plans may be developed and implemented for computer and information systems hardware and software to provide for more secure computer network architectures;
- Computer systems recovery and restoration plans may be prepared to return computer systems to full functionality after an incident;
- Up-to-date cybersecurity techniques (e.g., firewalls, virus protection, anti-spyware protection, encryption, and user authentication) and software patches may be used on commercial facility computer systems. Control systems can be isolated from the Internet where it is practical to do so;
- Redundancies in computer hardware and software can be used to permit the continued operation of information systems should the primary systems become disabled;
- Redundancies for control systems could also include the use of operators and manual controls for the system in the event of disruption. Offsite backup facilities can ensure the operation of control systems in the event of total failure at the primary sites; and
- Procedural and managerial requirements may be developed to include changing control and firewall monitoring, firewall assurance, standards, and training.

Redundancy

- Redundancy and emergency backup capabilities can be implemented to provide critical utility services (e.g., backup electric power generators and multiple utility feeder lines). When feasible, redundant and backup equipment may be stored in a different part of the facility than the primary supply equipment.

Structural Retrofit

- Harden, fortify, or modify the asset to reduce its vulnerability to attack or the likelihood of failure from a natural event.

5.1.7 Coordination of Sector Protective Programs

Owners and operators within the Dams Sector have widely diverse assets and missions. Accordingly, protective programs implemented within the Dams Sector vary because of different and distinct sector asset characteristics, operational processes, business environments, and risk management approaches. As previously described, sector assets range considerably in size (e.g., normal reservoir storage can range from a few acre-feet to 30 million acre-feet and levee systems can cover many miles); function (e.g., irrigation, hydroelectric power generation, water supply storage, flood control, navigation, fisheries, recreation, and sediment and hazardous materials control); and potential impacts (e.g., international, national, regional, and local) in the event that the asset is compromised.

Individual owners and operators have developed a variety of protective programs and resilience strategies within the Dams Sector. Given the complexity of assets within the sector, however, overarching processes or tools have not yet been agreed on as sector-accepted methods for identifying, cataloging, and validating sector needs or identifying and mitigating gaps in a sector-wide protective program. Obstacles to coordinating sector-wide protective programs include the large number and diversity of assets, security postures, and owners and operators; the diverse locations of many of the sector's assets; the limited availability of local law enforcement in many rural areas; and the differences in the definition of critical assets.

The SSA and its CIKR partners address these challenges through a coordinated national effort to develop guidance and reference materials related to protective programs and resilience strategies that are applicable to a wide range of sector assets. The SSA will identify sector-wide priorities associated with the Nation's most critical assets, taking into account their unique characteristics and operations. Noncritical sector assets could also benefit by incorporating any relevant measures and recommendations that are aligned with the sector-wide priorities. DHS can assist the Dams Sector in exploring resource alternatives to enable the implementation of protective programs and resilience strategies that can benefit the emergency response capabilities of the surrounding communities through initiatives such as the BZPP. This DHS-administered grant program is designed to help local law enforcement and owners and operators increase security in the "buffer zone"—the area outside of a facility that can be used by an adversary to conduct surveillance or launch an attack. This program also provides owners and operators with an opportunity to identify potential means through which they can enhance security and protection capabilities.

The adequacy, sufficiency, and effectiveness of the sector's approach to protective programs can be determined as the result of a sector-wide risk assessment that takes into account, at a minimum, those assets considered to be critical since these assets provide the most significant contribution to the sector risk profile. The Dams SSA will coordinate and assist these efforts as appropriate and will seek the voluntary input of any relevant information that could support this sector-wide evaluation. The goal is to foster and support the appropriate collaboration mechanisms with all sector CIKR partners to evaluate the overall protection and resilience posture of the sector and identify sector-wide protection priorities.

5.2 Determining the Need for Protective Programs and Resilience Strategies

An effective asset protective program incorporates a well thought out and coordinated plan of action to deter, detect, delay, assess, and respond to attacks on sector assets, as well as to respond to, mitigate, and recover from such attacks or natural hazards as quickly and cost-effectively as possible in a manner that limits the direct consequences and minimizes the long-term impacts. Protective programs also need to be efficient; they must address real protective program needs in a cost-effective manner.

The common and industry-adopted approach for defining the appropriate protective measures against manmade attacks and natural hazards is to conduct a thorough and complete risk assessment. Risk assessment results are used in determining the thresholds for action, identifying gaps, evaluating whether closing the gap is possible, and prioritizing and determining the order in which protection gaps are addressed.

Risk assessments can be conducted at multiple levels (e.g., facility-specific, sector-wide, or cross-sector), and their scope defines the type of protective programs or resilience strategies that can be implemented. For example, the design of site-specific security measures by an owner or operator needs to be informed by the appropriate facility-specific assessment, which explicitly takes into account site vulnerabilities. On the other hand, the relative importance of sector-wide protective programs addressing a specific attack scenario can be assessed based on sector-level analysis.

Typically, the asset owner/operator's business case will govern what measures are included in its protective program. Owners and operators increasingly have recognized that disruption or destruction can have a significant impact on operational survivability, shareholder value, customer relations, and public confidence. However, security costs have grown considerably over recent years and additional investment in protection can increase those costs. Additional investments may not be considered necessary, particularly for events that owners and operators believe may never occur. Therefore, the protective measures developed by the SSA and its sector partners to respond to protective program needs or gaps must be based on an accurate assessment of the need for the measure or the threshold required for its implementation. Identified gaps also should be ranked in order of their significance, with high-priority gaps being addressed first. Protective measures also must be cost-effective.

To evaluate the need for protective programs and resilience strategies that address the most relevant cybersecurity issues associated with disruptions to control systems, Dams Sector partners are collaboratively developing a "Roadmap to Secure Control Systems in the Dams Sector" to provide a comprehensive framework and recommended strategies to promote the security and protection of control systems. The roadmap will enhance the sector's understanding and management of cyber risks, facilitate the identification of practical risk mitigation solutions, promote information sharing, and improve sector-wide awareness of cybersecurity concerns.

As described in Section 5.1.2, the SSA supports the development and implementation of protective programs and resilience strategies with a sector-wide focus. This can be achieved based on conditional risk considerations (considering vulnerability and consequences for generic attack vectors) that offer extremely useful insight into the types of attacks that could affect large segments of the sector or its subsectors, or the types of assets that could be associated with the highest risk for specific attack vectors.

Chapter 1 discusses the characteristics of the measures that the SSA and its CIKR partners will focus on to implement asset-specific or sector-wide protective programs that minimize resource demands. As repeated here, the effort will focus on protective measures that are as follows:

- Simple to implement, with low cost and high effectiveness;

- Consistent with effective business practices and shared among stakeholders using industry and trade association communication mechanisms;

- Based on cost-sharing incentives, market systems, and other means that will encourage private sector participation;

- Built on current practices that have been proven to be effective;

- Applicable across assets while allowing owners and operators to select the most appropriate method for their particular needs;

- Reliant on self-assessments, where appropriate; and

- Consistent with the risk profile and commensurate with the threat environment from an all-hazards perspective.

Where feasible, existing regulations and standards will be applied to close gaps. Measures for filling protective program gaps will be developed to ensure that they are aligned with current Bureau of Reclamation, USACE, and FERC guidelines or requirements in order to avoid adversely impacting their responsibilities. Asset owners and operators will select and implement protective measures that are consistent with their level of tolerable risk and the associated cost-benefit analyses.

5.3 Implementing Protective Programs and Resilience Strategies

Implementing a protective program involves the commitment of resources in the form of people, equipment, materials, time, and money. Implementation can involve installing protective measures that are permanent and thus become the routine, normal, or baseline conditions for providing everyday protection of an asset. Other implementation strategies may involve installing temporary protective measures only during times of a heightened security posture. Contingency plans (e.g., response plans, continuity-of-operations plans, pandemic plans, cyber incident response plans, and emergency action plans) are often crucially important components of protective programs and resilience strategies.

Asset owners and operators are responsible for implementing and maintaining their corresponding facility-specific programs and strategies. Owners and operators contribute to the improvement of the overall security, safety, and resilience of the sector by implementing protective measures that are consistent with the corresponding relative risk and are appropriate considering the corresponding dependencies and interdependencies with other sectors (e.g., the Energy, Water, and Transportation Systems Sectors; see Appendix 7). Consistent with their unique assets, operational processes, business environments, and risk management approaches, owners and operators could consider the following actions:

- Perform risk assessments using consistent methodologies that are compatible with their business environments and risk management approaches;
- Implement security measures based on the results of their risk assessments using effective practices within regulatory and agency requirements;
- Complete and use risk assessment information to evaluate the effectiveness of existing protective measures against specified threats;
- Develop security plans addressing both physical and cyber elements based on risk assessment results;
- Develop emergency action plans;
- Develop cyber threat response plans;
- Develop continuity-of-operations plans;
- Develop mitigation and disaster recovery plans;
- Develop and implement a personnel screening program; and
- Implement NERC CIP standards, as required, for their assets.

The amount of funding needed to implement protective measures across the sector will vary depending on the asset and the threat type. To ensure the most cost-efficient use of limited funds, sector partners typically will perform cost-benefit analyses to determine the best way to reduce their risks for a given threat. This process facilitates balancing the potential reduction in known risk against the feasibility and affordability of the protective measure to determine the return on investment.

In keeping with the Dams Sector's goal to provide guidance on managing risks, the SSA, in conjunction with the Dams Sector Security Education Workgroup, prepared a series of reference documents to assist owners and operators in implementing their protective programs:

- *Security Awareness Handbook*—Assists in identifying security concerns, coordinating proper response, and establishing effective partnerships with local law enforcement and first responder communities. A companion, nonsensitive guide was developed to allow for wider dissemination.
- *Protective Measures Handbook*—Assists in selecting protective measures to address the physical, cyber, and human elements, including recommendations for developing site security plans.

- *Crisis Management Handbook*—Provides information related to emergency response and preparedness issues, including recommendations for developing emergency action plans and recovery plans.

- *Security Awareness Guide for Levees*—Assists in identifying security concerns, surveillance indicators, and incident reporting.

- *Active and Passive Vehicle Barriers Guide*—Provides general information on active and passive vehicle barrier systems and their design and selection.

- *Waterside Barriers Guide*—Provides information on waterside barriers and their use, maintenance, and effectiveness.

- *Personnel Screening Guide*—Provides information that assists in developing and implementing personnel screening protocols.

- *Physical Security Measures for Levees Brochure*—Provides general information on physical security measures that are applicable to levees.

- *Security Awareness for Levee Owners Brochure*—Provides succinct information on security issues that are relevant to levee owners.

Regional pilot efforts, such as the Dams Sector Exercise Series (DSES), also provide an effective mechanism for the development and implementation of resilience strategies at the regional level. DSES consists of regional exercises involving multiple facilities, agencies, and jurisdictions that may be affected by the same group of hazards. The overarching goal of these efforts is to develop a strategy for improving regional resilience and preparedness that, while directly applicable to the initial system under consideration, is "scalable" in the sense that resulting processes and solutions may be extrapolated to larger regions with similar characteristics.

Focusing efforts on mitigating the outcomes of attacks increases the number of possible approaches to include a wider set of options, many of which are less sensitive to threat uncertainty than the traditional prevention-centric approaches. When not constrained to adding additional layers of security or trying to obtain better threat information, decisionmakers can develop and implement measures that may be more effective against a wide variety of future threats, and can potentially do so at a lower overall cost. Consequence mitigation approaches are less sensitive to uncertainty because, in many cases, they provide tangible protection even in the absence of knowledge about the nature of an attack, the attackers, or from where the threat is coming.[17]

5.4 Monitoring Program Performance

Facility-specific protective programs are monitored and evaluated by the corresponding asset owners and regulatory agencies to determine if they are effective, have closed the identified protective program gaps that they were intended to address, and can be improved. This ongoing assessment is an important element of an asset's overall business case for maintaining or improving its protective posture.

Similarly, the Dams SSA continuously evaluates sector-wide protective programs and resilience strategies to determine their effectiveness in achieving the desired objectives identified by the sector. As part of this effort, and because of its significant influence on the sector risk profile, the Dams SSA will periodically reassess the process used to identify critical assets and confirm that it is actually capturing the full range of assets whose failure or disruption could potentially lead to the most severe impacts from a sector perspective. Protective programs and resilience strategies will be assessed by considering their impact on those elements that constitute the main risk drivers.

---

[17] Brian A. Jackson, *Marrying Prevention and Resilience Balancing Approaches to an Uncertain Terrorist Threat*, RAND Corporation, 2008.

6. Measure Effectiveness

Figure 6-1: Measuring Effectiveness

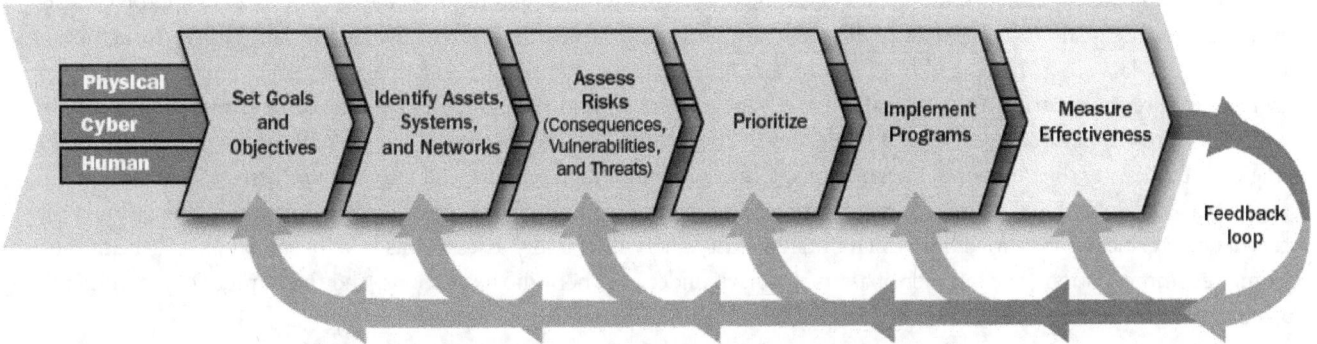

Figure 6-1: Measuring Effectiveness

Continuous improvement to enhance protection of CIKR

Measuring the overall effectiveness of Dams Sector protective programs and resilience strategies described in Section 5.1 requires identifying, describing, and measuring the outcomes of their corresponding risk mitigation activities (RMAs). This chapter describes how the Dams Sector identifies these activities, provides several examples, and explains the system used to measure their effectiveness in order to support continuous improvement in its protection and resilience efforts.

6.1 Risk Mitigation Activities

Risk mitigation activities are programs, tools, or initiatives that directly or indirectly reduce risk in the sector and/or enhance the sector's resilience. The Dams Sector features multiple RMAs that are consistent with the sector goals and corresponding risk profile, and that are implemented through a number of different stakeholders, including owners and operators, regulatory agencies, and the Dams Sector SSA.

Some risk mitigation activities may apply only to specific segments within the sector, either by function (e.g., navigation projects), ownership (e.g., Bureau of Reclamation-owned facilities), or regulatory framework (e.g., FERC-regulated projects). RMAs can also be drawn from cross-sector protective programs (e.g., cybersecurity standards for bulk electric power producers). Examples of risk mitigation activities that derive from the protective programs and resilience strategies described in sections 5.1.3 and 5.1.4 are the Bureau of Reclamation's site security program, the FERC hydropower security program, and the NERC critical cyber asset identification standards.

Other risk mitigation activities have a sector-wide focus because they correspond to protective programs and resilience strategies that are generally applicable across the Dams Sector and are not limited to a specific owner, regulatory jurisdiction, or facility type. Some of the initiatives conducted by the Dams Sector SSA, such as the systematic identification of critical assets though the CTS methodology or the implementation of regional exercises, are examples of RMAs with a sector-wide focus.

6.2 Process for Measuring Effectiveness

Accurately and expeditiously measuring program effectiveness requires well-designed and efficiently gathered progress indicators. Such indicators contribute to establishing accountability, documenting actual performance, facilitating diagnoses, promoting effective management, and providing feedback—all of which contribute to continued improvement in protective programs and resilience strategies.

6.2.1 Process for Measuring Sector Progress

Assessing risk mitigation activities and their supporting programs and strategies requires the development of appropriate progress indicators. The goals and objectives of the protective program or resilience strategy dictate the data gathered and frame the forms in which data are gathered and from whom, and how they are reported. For example, the goal of a protective program may be to ensure the security of the critical assets within an owner's portfolio; an objective may be to ensure the security of those assets through periodic security and vulnerability assessments. Consequently, the agency will complete a screening, such as the CTS, to identify the number of critical assets, followed by thorough security and vulnerability assessments of the critical assets, to catalog any risk reduction recommendations. Corresponding program progress indicators could be the number of assets deemed critical, the number for which initial security and vulnerability assessments have been completed, the number of ensuing recommendations, the number of assets that have undergone periodic inspections, and the number of recommendations that have been closed out.

As illustrated in the previous example, progress indicators can take a number of forms; however, they must clearly state what is being measured and the data must be objective and reasonably available. Progress indicators can be outcome metrics, output data, or descriptive data.

Outcome metrics are measures that indicate the progress, value, or *beneficial results* toward achieving a strategic goal and the associated target rather than the level of activity. A high-level metric may demonstrate national achievement of risk mitigation as a result of implementation of a particular CIKR protection initiative.

Output (or process) data are used to gauge whether specific activities were performed as planned, track the progress of a task, or report on the output of a process. Output data show progress toward performing the activities necessary to achieve CIKR protection goals and can serve as leading indicators for outcome measures. They also help build a comprehensive picture of CIKR protection status and activities. Descriptive data are used to understand sector resources and activities, but do not reflect CIKR protection performance. Examples include a narrative description of progress and the number of facilities and critical facilities in an owner's portfolio.

Owners and operators are responsible for assessing the performance of their respective programs. The Dams Sector Programs and Metrics Workgroup will assist in the development of relevant progress indicators to assess the benefits of sector-wide risk mitigation activities.

6.2.2 Information Collection and Verification

Sector stakeholders are responsible for collecting and verifying progress indicator information and data for their respective programs. The Dams Sector SSA assumes these responsibilities for risk mitigation activities that are sector-wide in nature. Because the sector's goals and objectives encompass its vision of a safe, secure, and resilient posture that incorporates physical, cyber, and human elements, the protective programs developed to achieve that posture are naturally linked to one or several of the sector's goals listed in Section 1.3.

Due to the potentially sensitive nature of data requested as part of the information collection and verification described in this section, Federal and State regulatory agencies are obliged to ensure that requested information can be afforded the appropriate levels of protection from disclosure. The promulgation of the PCII rule may allow the private sector to provide the requested information to DHS voluntarily or to its conforming Federal and State partners. In the absence of such procedural protection, data collection from the private sector will be problematic.

6.2.3 Reporting

Pursuant to HSPD-7, the SSA will report annually to the Secretary of Homeland Security on sector progress in implementing protective programs and resilience strategies by the development of the Dams Sector Annual Report. The SSA will share the sector annual report with CIKR partners through available information-sharing mechanisms.

6.3 Using Metrics for Continuous Improvement

The use of outcome metrics, output data, and descriptive data to compare performance to goals allows the SSA and its CIKR partners to adjust and adapt their and the sector's CIKR protection approach to account for progress achieved and for changes in threats and other relevant environments. As protective programs are implemented, the consequences and vulnerabilities associated with the assets will be affected. Accordingly, Dams Sector and national risk profiles must be reviewed routinely to help inform current and prospective allocation of resources in light of recently implemented protective actions or other factors. These other factors can include such items as an increased understanding of potential system-wide cascading consequences or new threat intelligence.

The dynamic nature of the Dams Sector risk profile may potentially require the updating or modification of sector goals, objectives, and associated metrics. Concern regarding the impact on CIKR partners of data gathering and reporting or the adequacy of the data to measure the progress of the sector could also trigger the need for this review. The SSA, in active collaboration with the sector councils, will coordinate the periodic review of sector goals, objectives, and associated metrics to evaluate their relevance and assess the need for modification.

7. CIKR Protection Research and Development

Owners, operators, and regulators of the sector's dams have a wealth of experience and knowledge on the safe design, construction, operation, and maintenance of these assets. However, the Dams Sector recognizes the need to better understand the threats, vulnerabilities, consequences, and subsequent risks associated with these assets. Sector partners have pursued R&D in these topics for the past several years, with a focus on the vulnerabilities of concrete and embankment dams.

Dams Sector partners implemented security improvements for high-risk and high-consequence facilities even before the September 11th attacks. In addition to numerous effective practices developed and implemented by asset owners and operators, many organizations within the sector collaborated in several relevant R&D initiatives, including the development of computer-based tools such as the Anti-Terrorist Planner for Dams by USACE, and numerical and experimental modeling of blast effects on dams and appurtenant structures by the Bureau of Reclamation and USACE.

This chapter explains how R&D considerations are incorporated into a coordinated plan to benefit the Dams Sector. It describes sector partners' roles in identifying R&D needs and requirements by determining if they are being met through R&D efforts within or beyond the sector and then prioritizing any unmet needs. The chapter concludes with the sector's management strategy for its R&D requirements.

7.1 Overview of Sector R&D

Recognizing the role of R&D in reducing risk within the sector, the sector councils identified enhancing the security and resilience of the Dams Sector through R&D efforts as a sector goal. The SSA and Dams Sector R&D Workgroup, composed of GCC and SCC members, lead the activities to characterize sector research and technology needs, maintain awareness of the state-of-the-art technology and research related to those needs, and delineate the gaps between what is needed and what is available or known in order to coordinate R&D activities.

Sector-wide coordination of R&D activities cannot be executed in a vacuum. The current and future R&D work of the DHS Science and Technology Directorate (S&T), other Federal agencies, and the National Dam Safety Program are taken into account to leverage multiple investments across the sector and thus avoid duplicative efforts. An example is the inclusion of an R&D capability gap titled "Rapid Condition Assessment and Strengthening of Levees" in the 2009 Dams Sector Annual Report. This identified need supports and builds on the initial research of USACE and DHS S&T, and the recommendation of the National Committee on Levee Safety calling for development of a federally funded R&D program to develop innovative technologies for repairs and improved engineering methods that would lead to more reliable levees and more cost-effective approaches to their safety and resilience.

7.2 Sector R&D Requirements

The National Critical Infrastructure Protection R&D Plan (NCIP R&D Plan) contains nine themes that are applicable to all 18 CIKR sectors and are as follows:

- Detection and sensor systems;
- Protection and prevention;
- Entry and access portals;
- Insider threats;
- Analysis and decision support systems;
- Response and recovery tools;
- New and emerging threats and vulnerabilities;
- Advanced infrastructure architectures and systems design; and
- Human and social issues.

R&D gaps and needs are systematically identified through the Sector Annual Report process, and are therefore updated as needed in each subsequent report. Detailed information on each gap is also included in the Dams Sector Annual Report to aid DHS IP and S&T, and the White House Office of Science and Technology Policy (OSTP) in their update of the annual NCIP R&D Plan. This information includes related Dams Sector goals, the corresponding critical infrastructure protection R&D theme, the gap description, the description of operational requirements, identification of end users, and identification of existing related capabilities or technologies.

Through the process cited above and based on the annual evaluation of sector-wide efforts, the SSA and R&D Workgroup refine the sector gaps. The Dams Sector R&D capability gaps, as reported in the 2009 Dams Sector Annual Report, are as follows:

- Validated blast damage prediction tools for embankment dams and levees;
- Validated blast damage prediction tools for concrete dams, gates, and appurtenant structures;
- Effective blast mitigation technologies;
- Emergency closure devices and rapid breach repair technologies;
- Integrated waterside detection and deterrence systems;
- Validated aircraft impact damage prediction tools; and
- Rapid condition assessment and strengthening of levees.

These capability gaps address the following NCIP R&D themes: detection and sensor systems, protection and prevention, analysis and decision support systems, and response and recovery tools.

7.3 Sector R&D Plan

Coordination of the R&D efforts is accomplished through the collaborative efforts of the SSA and the R&D Workgroup who evaluate current Federal research initiatives, compare them to the sector capability gaps, and identify those research programs that have the potential for successfully meeting those needs. The requirements not met by current efforts are clearly identified and thoroughly described, prioritized, and documented through the Dams Sector Annual Report development process.

The sector R&D gaps and technology needs are forwarded to DHS S&T and OSTP to match these gaps with the requirements identified by other CIKR sectors and potentially identify any cross-sector opportunities for collaboration.

Sector gaps and needs are selected and prioritized based on the risks to sector assets that have not yet been adequately addressed, but that have the potential to be resolved to the point that the risk can be disproven as a valid threat or managed or mitigated through physical or operational interventions that are cost-effective and operationally acceptable. Several of the sector gaps and needs require the development of a fundamental understanding of the blast effects on a variety of surfaces and materials, and the analytical methods to understand modes of damage before effective and affordable mitigation or management measures can be developed.

The Dams Sector is currently identifying R&D needs associated with the security and resilience of control systems. R&D will serve to improve the sector's cybersecurity protective capabilities and dramatically lower the cost of existing solutions so that State, local, tribal, and territorial governments and private sector partners can afford to do more with their limited budgets.

7.4 R&D Management Processes

Under the overall coordination provided by the SSA, the Dams Sector developed and will maintain a collaborative framework for determining the new technical capabilities needed to achieve the sector's desired security and resilience end state and national goals, formulating coordinated efforts to develop new technologies, and facilitating the leveraging of R&D efforts in such a way that the new technologies can benefit the sector as a whole.

The Dams Sector needs to continue its efforts to better understand the vulnerabilities, threats, and consequences that could result from manmade and natural hazards, and the potential protective measures and resilience strategies that could be implemented to mitigate the corresponding risks. This improved understanding is best achieved through additional research, studies, and analyses. The specific technology needs and requirements for the security and protection of sector assets will be developed by the R&D Workgroup in collaboration with the SSA through frequent and regular communication not only with sector partners, but also with DHS S&T and the National Cybersecurity Division (NCSD), and other relevant public and private R&D organizations. R&D Workgroup members will continue to collect and prioritize the technology and research requirements for the security, protection, and resilience of sector assets.

The workgroup will focus its efforts on identifying technology requirements that have the greatest impact on the Dams Sector and on exchanging information on these issues. This process will support those agencies and organizations directly involved in R&D initiatives relevant to the sector. Annual updates to the Dams Sector R&D capability gaps and recommendations for the adjustment of priorities will be coordinated by the SSA in conjunction with the R&D Workgroup. Concurrence with the recommended prioritization will be sought from sector partners through the GCC and SCC. The overall process will benefit from periodic updates to be provided by DHS S&T and OSTP on any advances in technology that may assist the Dams Sector, even if the research was not originally intended for the specific benefit of this sector.

The basic elements of the R&D management process are as follows:

- Adoption of strategic initiatives will be given the greatest consideration in the activities of the group;

- Development and review of sector technology requirements will be a consistent agenda item for the regularly scheduled meetings of the GCC and SCC through presentations of the R&D Workgroup;

- The SSA will work with the R&D Workgroup to serve as the initial point of contact and coordination between the GCC and other Federal agencies and representatives to the NCIP R&D Plan;

- The SSA and the R&D Workgroup will ensure that the research needs of the Dams Sector are included in the activities of DHS S&T and OSTP; will address the nine themes of the NCIP R&D Plan; and will ensure that initiatives and information generated by the processes of the plan are communicated back to the GCC, SCC, and other key stakeholders; and

- Additional input on the technology requirements of the Dams Sector will be obtained through the solicitation of ideas from other organizations and program involved with the safety of dams, levees, and related structures, such as the National Dam Safety Program chaired by FEMA.

7.4.1 Current R&D Initiatives

DHS S&T will furnish the SSA and the Dams Sector R&D Workgroup with a summary of the current and upcoming Federal R&D initiatives that have the potential to meet the security risk reduction requirements of sector assets. This list will include research identified by other CIKR sectors, many of which have similar research needs to those of the Dams Sector. This information will be shared with the sector councils and other organizations involved in the Dams Sector, as needed. This information will be critical for identifying the most effective mechanisms for obtaining or developing the technologies that can meet the primary needs of the sector. This communications process will promote collaboration among agencies, thus enabling many needs of the Dams Sector to be met by existing R&D without the expenditure of scarce funds and resources.

Many research initiatives are already underway within the Dams Sector to address key concerns on the vulnerabilities and protective measures associated with sector assets. Federal sector partners will provide the SSA with relevant information regarding current and planned R&D activities, as appropriate, to facilitate the compilation of the Dams Sector Annual Report.

The R&D Workgroup will compare current and upcoming Federal research initiatives to the Dams Sector technology needs and identify research programs that have the highest likelihood of successfully meeting those needs. The workgroup will also identify, prioritize, and document any needs of the Dams Sector that are not being met. This information will be furnished through the SSA to the sector councils and, with their approval, will eventually be sent back to DHS S&T and OSTP to match these gaps to other CIKR sectors and identify any opportunities for an initiative sponsored by other sectors to support the needs of the Dams Sector. This process will help to ensure a focused and effective R&D investment on the highest national CIKR protection priorities and identify multiple-use technology solutions.

7.4.2 Candidate R&D Initiatives

R&D programs already completed or underway, as identified through the CIKR protection R&D process, and that will meet the needs of the Dams Sector will be given the highest priority for tracking by the R&D Workgroup. This research should provide an immediate benefit to the Dams Sector and its results should be shared with sector partners. Because some of the research results may be sensitive or classified, the R&D Workgroup will work jointly with the Information Sharing Workgroup in identifying the appropriate processes for sharing the completed research results with all relevant parties.

Planned or future research initiatives identified by the CIKR protection R&D process or planned by Federal GCC members that will meet the needs of the Dams Sector will be given the next highest priority for tracking by the R&D Workgroup. The SSA will work with the R&D Workgroup, sector councils, and other CIKR partners to identify funding mechanisms, expertise to be applied, appropriate coordination processes, and other necessary resource requirements to ensure the successful completion of these research programs. A broad spectrum of sector R&D needs could be met through Federal Government initiatives conducted by or for other sectors. However, R&D topics specific to the Dams Sector can be met only through funding of a dedicated program developed and implemented in coordination with all sector partners.

8. Managing and Coordinating SSA Responsibilities

For many CIKR sectors, including the Dams Sector, developing and implementing a national plan that coordinates sector protective activities presents an ongoing challenge because of the scale and complexity of the sector. This chapter describes the management and coordination activities that have been and will continue to be performed to meet this challenge successfully. Specifically, this chapter explains how DHS will manage its SSA responsibilities and how the DSSP will be maintained and updated. It also describes sector reporting processes, resources and budgets, and protection training and educational needs. The chapter also includes a description of the sector partnership model and the plans for its ongoing enhancement and ends with a section on how sector information will be shared and protected.

8.1 Program Management Approach

This section describes how the SSA will staff and manage its NIPP-related responsibilities over the short and long terms. Pursuant to the NIPP, the SSA is responsible for working with DHS and government asset owners and regulators to implement the NIPP sector partnership model and risk management framework; develop protective programs, resilience strategies, and related requirements; and provide sector-level CIKR protection guidance in line with the overarching guidance established by DHS pursuant to HSPD-7. In accordance with HSPD-7, the SSA is also responsible for collaborating with private sector partners and encouraging the development of appropriate voluntary information-sharing and analysis mechanisms within the sector. This includes encouraging voluntary security-related information sharing, where possible, among private entities within the sector, as well as among public and private entities in general.

In addition, the Dams SSA will fulfill the SSA responsibilities previously described in this document and coordinate and manage development, implementation, maintenance, and modification of the DSSP.

In performing its responsibilities, the Dams SSA will work with entities both within DHS IP and outside DHS IP (e.g., NCSD, S&T, etc.) to leverage programs being conducted throughout DHS that could enhance the protective posture and resilience of the Dams Sector. The Dams SSA works within a DHS framework in which the DHS IP is the designated SSA for six CIKR sectors, including the Dams Sector. DHS IP manages the six sectors through the Sector-Specific Agency Executive Management Office (SSA EMO), which is described in greater detail in Appendix 8.

As described below, considerable cooperation and coordination among CIKR partners has occurred, including interaction between the private sector and all levels of government. Implementing this DSSP requires building on the strong relationships that exist today and fostering new relationships when appropriate.

8.2 Processes and Responsibilities

Maintaining and periodically updating the DSSP and reporting on the sector's progress in meeting its goals are among the SSA's responsibilities. Implementing the DSSP and supporting the sector's goals require sufficient resources and budgets, as well as appropriate training and educational opportunities.

8.2.1 SSP Maintenance and Updating

As the primary planning and management document for the Dams Sector, the DSSP must be maintained and updated appropriately. Similar to the NIPP, the DSSP will undergo a thorough triennial review in collaboration with Dams Sector CIKR partners. The SSA, which is responsible for version control of the document and is the only entity currently authorized to revise the document, will lead the triennial review.

In addition to the formal triennial review, the SSA will update the DSSP annually or on an ad hoc basis as warranted by changes in the sector's security posture or procedures. To ensure accuracy and reinforce the partnership nature of this effort, the SSA will coordinate DSSP revisions with Dams Sector CIKR partners. The full GCC and SCC, as well as State, local, tribal, and territorial representatives, subject matter experts (as appropriate), and IP leadership will review the document and provide substantive input. Suggested comments and changes will be adjudicated and revised drafts will be issued for additional review. The SSA coordinates all comments and maintains full version control over the document.

The SSA will work with the rest of DHS, other Federal agencies, State and local governments, tribal governments, the private sector, and other CIKR partners to collect information and build a comprehensive picture of Dams Sector infrastructure protection and resilience efforts across the Nation. This effort assists DHS in understanding how CIKR protection and resilience activities are being conducted, what priorities and requirements drive these activities, and how such activities are funded.

8.2.2 SSP Implementation Milestones

The NIPP risk management framework provides a logical basis for describing the actions that the SSA and CIKR partners will take in implementing this DSSP. Since the DSSP provides the underlying framework for the Dams Sector, the following actions are generally procedural in nature; activity details are provided in the sector annual report.

- **Set Goals and Objectives.** The sector's goals and objectives will be reviewed each year for relevance. The Dams Sector Program and Metrics Workgroup and the SSA will initiate the review; any changes will be subject to the approval of the sector councils.

- **Identify Assets, Systems, and Networks.** As noted in earlier sections, the NID is a very useful tool for identifying dams and the sector has a good understanding of the number of locks, but a reasonably accurate methodology for identifying levees is yet to be found. The same is somewhat true for identifying the sector's critical cyber assets and cyber functions. The sector will continue to work with USACE and other CIKR partners to promote the development of a comprehensive levee inventory. In addition, the sector will implement a cybersecurity roadmap that will facilitate the identification of critical cyber functions. Efforts will also be made to gain a more thorough understanding of the number and condition of industrial waste impoundments.

- **Assess Risks.** In collaboration with CIKR partners, the SSA will continue efforts to develop and implement a sector-wide conditional risk assessment methodology capable of taking into account the results of the wide variety of consequence and vulnerability assessment tools used in the sector. This can include activities to develop generally accepted loss of life, economic consequence, and vulnerability assessment definitions and methodologies.

- **Prioritize.** To realistically take the first step in prioritizing its assets, the sector will continue to refine the CTS approach to identify its highest consequence facilities. The CTS for levees will be refined in concert with the levee councils and its implementation will be coordinated with the levee inventory efforts by USACE and other levee stakeholders. Prioritization of assets will be further facilitated through the development and implementation of consequence and vulnerability assessment tools.

- **Implement Programs.** The SSA and sector asset owners and operators will develop risk-informed management activities that promote sector protective programs. These programs can include physical protective measures, modeling and analysis, and contingency planning. The SSA and its CIKR partners will pursue R&D initiatives that are responsive to the capability gaps identified by the sector.

- **Measure Effectiveness.** Progress indicators will be developed for the sector's risk mitigation activities in order to facilitate an annual evaluation of the activities' contributions to reducing risk, advancing protection, and enhancing sector resilience.

8.2.3 Resources and Budgets

No individual entity has authority over resources and budgets for the entire Dams Sector because of the variety of Federal, State, local, tribal, and private sector CIKR partners that contribute funds and other resources to the protection of sector assets. As a result, the SSA has limited information on how Dams Sector CIKR partners allocate resources for their security and resilience programs, and even less influence over how future resources should be allocated.

Within these limitations, the SSA will continue to work with its Dams Sector partners to gather resource and budget information. The SSA will develop and share recommendations with the Dams Sector CIKR partners regarding the allocation of sector resources and related funding on the basis of national priorities set forth in the NIPP and the DHS National Annual Report, sector priorities developed in support of the DSSP, and the sector CIKR annual report. Recommendations for resource or funding allocations will be based in large part on an analysis of the threats posed against the Dams Sector as a whole and the cost-effectiveness and reduction of risk associated with individual expenditure recommendations. These same sources will influence the SSA's sector-specific budget planning.

The SSA, in conjunction with other DHS offices and divisions as appropriate, is responsible for developing the recommended internal DHS annual budget requests for Dams Sector Federal expenditures. By September 1 of each year, the Dams SSA will submit its budget requests for the following fiscal year. Between September and November of each year, the Dams SSA, through proper DHS channels, will work with the Office of Management and Budget to provide any additional information that may be required to define DHS budget and resources available for Dams Sector security.

The SSA serves as the subject matter expert in reviewing and providing recommendations on specific internal target grant programs that may benefit the Dams Sector. The SSA will work closely with the private sector to promote the most efficient use of these Federal expenditures and will offer its expertise to assist the private sector in maximizing the utility of the resources that it uses for sector security.

8.2.4 Training and Education

Successful implementation of the national risk management framework relies on building and maintaining individual and organizational CIKR resilience and protection expertise. The NIPP continuum of CIKR capability development includes the following elements: outreach, awareness, education, training, and exercise. The Dams Sector and its CIKR partners rely on these formats to ensure the effective dissemination of information that promotes the sector's desired end state.

The SSA's and sector partner's participation in conferences and professional meetings provides information on NIPP, DHS, and Dams Sector programs and reference documents. Several sector council members represent professional organizations; these liaison relationships are particularly important because they facilitate bilateral information exchange and outreach.

These organizations and the SSA sponsor and support the development of professional training opportunities, workshops, and reference documents. In addition, many dam owners and operators periodically conduct comprehensive exercises of their emergency action plans and other contingency plans. The SSA annually sponsors a series of sector exercises with the goal of improving regional resilience and preparedness with an all-hazards focus. The exercises involve different regional settings and multiple facilities and jurisdictions. The first series of these exercises took place in 2008 (DSES-08), with the overall goal of testing interoperability and communication protocols among governmental and nongovernmental entities facing a catastrophic event involving multiple dams located within the same river basin in Missouri. In early 2009, the SSA, in collaboration with USACE, the Pacific Northwest Economic Region, and other Pacific Northwest region stakeholders, initiated another series of exercises (DSES-09) that focused on a major flood event affecting the Tri-Cities area in Washington State.

All Dams Sector partners can benefit from such training, exercise, outreach, and educational opportunities. Asset owners and operators and facility chief safety and security officers could benefit from training on such topics as risk assessment, risk management, cost-benefit analysis, and cybersecurity strategies. Training of this nature would be particularly valuable if it were performed by Federal personnel at an institution such as the Federal Law Enforcement Training Center in order to build personal relationships among Federal and private security personnel. Security officers and State and local law enforcement could benefit from training on protection- and response-related topics ranging from countersurveillance to vehicle searches. Red-teaming facilities (i.e., testing a facility's security measures using trained teams of simulated adversaries) can help asset owners and operators determine the effectiveness of their security programs and prepare staff to respond quickly and properly in the event of an actual incident.

Government officials focused on emergency services across sectors could benefit from specialized education regarding sector assets, their specific functions, upstream and downstream implications to population and infrastructure, and other knowledge unique to the Dams Sector. Multi-jurisdictional exercises involving government officials are extremely valuable opportunities for outreach and education. The SSA and other DHS functions that affect the Dams Sector will also benefit through these exercises, as well as through training in the regulatory and reporting systems and the operating climates under which sector assets function.

The Dams Sector will continue to support the conduct of exercises and, in concert with the Dams Sector Security Education Workgroup, develop reference documents related to asset security, protection, and resilience, including contingency planning.

The Security Education Workgroup has also led the development of online training modules based on the three sector handbooks (Security Awareness, Protective Measures, and Crisis Management) to provide sector stakeholders with information on security vulnerabilities, enhance their ability to assess the risks to their respective facilities, and improve their incident response capabilities.

This training initiative is of great importance since the sector is extremely large in scope and includes owners and operators with limited funding. As such, these individuals are often unable to attend conferences and training sessions to obtain state-of-the-practice information. The online training modules will help to ensure that all sector stakeholders have the information needed to assist them in enhancing security and ultimately reducing risk at their respective facilities. Upon successful completion of any of the three training modules, users will be provided with a certificate of completion for their records. In addition, the SSA will maintain a record of all who have completed the training for metrics purposes.

Many Dams Sector CIKR partners have already participated in a variety of the training and educational activities open to them; however, more could be done. As part of the DSSP implementation process, the SSA will work with its CIKR partners to identify and encourage participation in existing training and educational opportunities. Additionally, the SSA will work with those partners to identify any gaps in training or training opportunities and to develop ways in which these gaps can be filled to ensure that the necessary training and educational opportunities are available to and are being used by Dams Sector CIKR partners. Cybersecurity awareness and education is also a key area where targeted training would be valuable.

8.3 Implementing the Partnership Model

Chapter 1 of the SSP describes the specific organizational participants involved in the coordinated development and implementation of a robust and comprehensive CIKR protection and resilience strategy for the sector. The SSA works with these partners to support more focused initiatives targeting specific subsectors or issues of concern, as well as broader initiatives and strategies that foster partnership, coordination, information sharing, and risk management activities across the sector. In addition, the SSA works with public and private sector partners to ensure that international physical and cybersecurity issues with implications for the sector are properly addressed and coordinated. The NIPP sector partnership model is the overarching framework within which the broad CIKR partnership operates.

DHS established the Critical Infrastructure Partnership Advisory Council (CIPAC) in 2006 to facilitate effective coordination among Federal, State, local, tribal, and territorial governments, and between government and the private sector. CIPAC provides a forum that allows CIKR partners to engage in a broad range of critical infrastructure protection and resilience activities. The ongoing communication and coordination enabled by this broad public-private partnership are critical to the SSA's mission to manage its responsibilities for leading the unified effort to manage risk to the sector.

8.3.1 NIPP Coordinating Councils

The sector partnership model is the framework proposed in the NIPP to promote and facilitate sector and cross-sector planning, coordination, collaboration, and information sharing for CIKR protection involving all levels of government and private sector owners and operators. The model encourages formation of the GCCs to coordinate government efforts and the SCCs to coordinate private sector efforts. DHS provides guidance, tools, and support to enable these groups to work together to carry out their respective roles and responsibilities. The goal of these organizational structures, partnerships, and information-sharing networks is to establish the context, framework, and support for the activities required to implement and sustain the national CIKR protection effort.

8.3.2 Dams Sector Coordinating Council

Although organized bodies such as trade associations already exist within the Dams Sector, it is critical that the sector have a coordinating, representative mechanism in place to address protection and resilience issues related to sector assets and to communicate effectively with DHS and other Federal agencies. The SCC, which was established in May 2005, comprises private owners, representatives from major utility companies, non-Federal dam owners, and representatives from major industry associations. The SCC has been meeting on a quarterly basis. Its meetings are open to any non-Federal dam owner and/or operator and its members are listed below:

- Allegheny Energy
- Ameren Services Company
- American Electric Power
- Association of State Dam Safety Officials
- Association of State Floodplain Managers
- AVISTA Utilities
- CMS Energy
- Colorado River Energy Distributors Association
- Dominion Resources
- Duke Energy

- Exelon Corporation
- Hydro-Quebec
- National Association of Flood and Stormwater Management Agencies
- National Hydropower Association
- National Mining Association (ex officio member)
- National Water Resources Association
- New York City Department of Environmental Protection (ex officio member)
- New York Power Authority
- Ontario Power Generation
- Pacific Gas and Electric Company
- PPL Corporation
- Progress Energy
- Public Utility District 1 of Chelan County, Washington
- Scana Corporation
- Seattle City Light
- South Carolina Public Service Authority (Santee-Cooper)
- Southern California Edison (ex officio member)
- Southern Company Generation
- United States Society on Dams
- Xcel Energy

The SCC has established the following mission:

> The Dams SCC serves as the private sector interface with the Federal Government on issues related to the security of dams, locks, and levees. Its primary purpose is to determine the nature of the risks posed against dams and related structures so that appropriate and timely information, as well as mitigation strategies, can be provided to the entities responsible for the operation and protection of those assets. The Dams SCC also serves as the principal asset owner interface with other private critical infrastructure sectors, as well as with DHS, FERC, other government agencies, and the GCC established to address issues related to the security of dams, locks, and levees.

The chair of the SCC represents the Dams Sector in the Partnership for Critical Infrastructure Security, which is the cross-sector coordination council for all 18 CIKR sectors. SCC members serve on National Infrastructure Advisory Council workgroups.

8.3.3 Levee Sub-Sector Coordinating Council

The LSCC, a component of the SCC, was established in February 2008. Its members are levee owners and representatives from professional organizations. The chair is appointed by NAFSMA; the vice chair is appointed by ASFPM.

LSCC members conduct quarterly meetings and attend classified briefings and other meetings with DHS and other government officials. The LSCC provides training and other outreach materials to levee owners and operators to assist them in establishing effective security and resilience programs and input to DHS on security and risk management issues related to levees.

The mission of the LSCC is to provide a forum in which levee owners and associations representing owners, such as NAFSMA and ASFPM, can collaborate with DHS and other Federal entities on matters related to the security and protection of levees. As a subcouncil to the SCC, the LSCC closely coordinates its efforts with those of the SCC.

Members of the LSCC are as follows:

- American Society of Civil Engineers (ex officio)
- Association of State Floodplain Managers
- FM Global (ex officio)
- Los Angeles County Department of Public Works
- Louisiana State Police, Levee District
- Metropolitan Water District of Southern California
- National Association of Flood and Stormwater Management Agencies
- Reclamation District 1000, Sacramento, CA
- South Florida Water Management District
- South La Foursche Levee District, Galiano, LA
- Southeast Louisiana Flood Protection Authority
- United States Society on Dams

8.3.4 Dams Sector Government Coordinating Council

The GCC, which was established in January 2005, acts as the counterpart and partner to the SCC to plan, implement, and execute sector-wide security programs for the sector's assets.

The GCC accomplishes its objectives through the following activities:

- Identifying issues that require public-private coordination and communication. The GCC brings together diverse Federal and State interests to identify and develop collaborative strategies that advance CIKR protection;
- Identifying needs and gaps in plans, programs, policies, procedures, and strategies;
- Acknowledging and recognizing successful programs and practices. The GCC facilitates the sharing of experiences, ideas, effective practices, and innovative approaches related to CIKR protection; and
- Leveraging complementary resources within government and between government and industry.

The GCC meets on a quarterly basis. The member agencies that make up the GCC are as follows:

- Bonneville Power Administration
- U.S. Department of Agriculture, Natural Resources Conservation Service
- U.S. Department of Commerce, National Weather Service
- U.S. Department of Energy
- U.S. Department of Defense, U.S. Army Corps of Engineers

- U.S. Department of Homeland Security, Federal Emergency Management Agency, Office of Infrastructure Protection, Science and Technology Directorate, and U.S. Coast Guard
- U.S. Department of the Interior, Bureau of Reclamation
- U.S. Department of Labor, Mine Safety and Health Administration
- U.S. Department of State, International Boundary and Water Commission
- U.S. Environmental Protection Agency
- Federal Energy Regulatory Commission
- Tennessee Valley Authority
- State governments, including the State Dam Safety Offices of California, Colorado, Nebraska, New Jersey, North Carolina, Ohio, Pennsylvania, and Washington

The Bureau of Indian Affairs, a DOI agency, works with Native American Tribes to operate and maintain its high- and significant-hazard potential dams on reservations. The Bureau of Reclamation serves as the primary representative for all DOI bureaus and agencies on the GCC.

8.3.5 Levee Sub-Sector Government Coordinating Council

The LGCC, a component of the GCC, is the counterpart to the LSCC. The objective of the LGCC is to provide a forum for effective coordination of protection activities related to levees and flood risk reduction infrastructure systems among Federal and State agencies. The LGCC will accomplish this objective based on the following activities:

- Identifying critical infrastructure issues related to levees and flood risk reduction infrastructure systems in general that require public-private coordination and communication;
- Evaluating and assessing interdependencies;
- Identifying solutions to mitigate consequences, reduce regional impacts, and enhance recovery capabilities in order to increase overall resilience;
- Identifying and promoting successful resilience-enhancing programs and practices;
- Leveraging resources across the government to develop and implement consistent and risk-commensurate protective programs;
- Supporting and complementing levee safety and flood risk management efforts at the national and regional levels; and
- Identifying and prioritizing levee R&D requirements.

LGCC member agencies include:

- California Department of Water Resources
- U.S. Department of Agriculture, Natural Resources Conservation Service
- U.S. Department of Defense, U.S. Army Corps of Engineers
- U.S. Department of Homeland Security, Federal Emergency Management Agency and the Office of Infrastructure Protection
- U.S. Department of State, International Boundary and Water Commission

The LGCC is chaired by USACE.

8.4 Information Sharing and Protection

The security and resilience of the Dams Sector can be advanced through information sharing among CIKR partners and with DHS with regard to threats, vulnerabilities, and lessons learned. Conveying this information often requires adequately protecting it from inappropriate disclosure.

To ensure effective information-sharing practices, while also protecting sensitive information from the general public, the Dams Sector, through guidance provided by the Information Sharing Workgroup, established an information-sharing environment (ISE) through which sector stakeholders can collaborate and exchange information pertaining to prevention, readiness, security, resilience, and recovery issues within the Dams Sector. This framework is the primary means by which the sector communicates all information, including that related to threat, vulnerability, and lessons learned.

The Dams Sector ISE comprises trusted and vetted sector stakeholders. Agencies and organizations recognized as members of the Dams Sector councils constitute the core of the Dams Sector ISE, which will be concentrically expanded to include all relevant sector stakeholders.

8.4.1 Information-Sharing Mechanisms

Successful protective programs and effective resilience strategies depend on a clear definition of the threat and the corresponding site vulnerabilities. Historical patterns for manmade threats indicate some commonalities and trends in the use of tactics. However, these tactics evolve constantly as protective measures are installed or other parts of the protective posture are adopted at a site. As a result, the threat often changes; weapons, tools, and tactics formerly used against a particular target now might be used against new targets. Manmade threat tactics and their associated tools, weapons, and use of explosives serve as the basis for the design for any protective measures that encompass the protective program.

Defining and understanding the threat and its objectives and desired outcomes are key requirements and are essential to designing an effective protective system that encompasses the overall program. Sharing information on delineated threats can help enhance sector security and resilience and several organizations have developed such protocols.

USACE has been sharing information related to suspicious activity at dams with Federal dam owners and the collective homeland security community since November 2001. USACE shares this information via the Incident Reporting System, which resides on the USACE corporate emergency management system, ENGLink Interactive. This tool is a dynamic information-sharing system with the following functions: user-friendly data entry of threatening or suspicious activity and criminal activity; geospatial mapping of activity; general posting of situation reports; file attachment capabilities (e.g., digital media); permission to revise, modify, and/or update reporting; immediate dissemination of e-mail alerts; and a communications check status for command and control purposes. This incident reporting system is used by various agencies in developing intelligence reports.

Federal partners leverage this incident reporting system to report suspicious activities. Select members meet monthly to review events, conduct preliminary analysis of reported events, and produce scheduled activity summaries. Product summaries are not only distributed within sector organizations, but also to selected agencies in the DHS intelligence and law enforcement communities for aggregate analysis.

On a concurrent path, the development of HITRAC facilitated direct dialogue between the DHS intelligence branch and individual asset owners. A HITRAC representative is assigned to the Dams Sector and meets regularly with the SCC and GCC and provides periodic briefings at the classified level.

In 2005, the Dams Sector established the Information Sharing Workgroup, which serves as the sector information-sharing steward. The workgroup actively addresses multiple issues related to information sharing across the sector. The Dams Sector is unusual in that there are Federal, State, and private owners and operators of assets. The workgroup's goal is to navigate the issues surrounding information sharing among such a broad spectrum to benefit all owners and operators. Although much has been accomplished with regard to defining the information-sharing procedures, there are still challenges to be overcome.

> The continued utilization of the HSIN-CS Dams Portal as the primary information-sharing mechanism contributes to enhanced situational awareness across the sector. The Dams Sector continues to engage additional organizations and agencies that would benefit from having access to the portal and identify ways to improve the capabilities of the HSIN-CS Dams Portal.

The Dams Sector designated the HSIN-CS Dams Portal as the sector's primary information-sharing mechanism. This portal is an effective Web-based tool through which trusted and vetted public and private sector partners, including owners and operators, can obtain sensitive but unclassified information that is relevant to a number of sector issues. To ensure that this Web-based system provides the required capabilities to effectively share information, the portal was developed to emulate the structure of the Dams Sector ISE.

The United States Computer Emergency Readiness Team (US-CERT) also provides an important information-sharing mechanism through its Web-based portal. US-CERT was established in 2003 to help secure the Nation's Internet infrastructure and coordinate defenses against and responses to cyber attacks across the Nation. US-CERT is responsible for analyzing and reducing cyber threats and vulnerabilities, disseminating cyber threat warning information, and coordinating cyber incident response activities. US-CERT also assists in the management, response, and handling of incidents, vulnerabilities, and mitigation of threat actions specific to critical control systems functions. The Industrial Control System Cyber Emergency Readiness Team is a special section of US-CERT that was specifically created to coordinate global efforts and response to cyber vulnerabilities and threats that affect industrial control systems.

The sector's participation in efforts such as the Cross-Sector Cybersecurity Working Group and the Industrial Control System Joint Working Group provides additional opportunities for effective information sharing on critical issues related to cybersecurity.

8.4.2 Sharing Lessons Learned

Notwithstanding their legitimate concerns regarding information sharing within the sector and with DHS, the sector's CIKR partners share lessons learned with the understanding that their dissemination is properly controlled as needed. The primary vehicles for conveying lessons learned are the sector-produced reference documents and the HSIN-CS Dams Portal.

The reference documents and their Web-based training formats are based on topics that the sector deems important (e.g., awareness of possible surveillance being conducted at a facility, the elements of a protective program, the escalation of protective measures as the threat increases, and contingency planning to increase mission resilience). Similarly, owners and operators post documents, templates, and model forms on the HSIN-CS Dams Portal that can be used by others.

The publicly available reference documents and information on gaining access to the HSIN-CS Dams Portal are disseminated through professional conferences and meetings, training programs, and sector members' Web sites.

8.4.3 Protecting Sensitive Information

The sensitivities associated with revealing any potential facility-specific vulnerabilities are obvious and preclude wide dissemination within the sector. Facility owners and operators must comply with their respective agencies' or organization's information security policies. Owners and operators of privately held assets are particularly concerned that some of the highly sensitive facility-specific information shared with DHS may not be adequately covered by the protections offered through the PCII framework.

Although the sector maintains a preference for unlimited distribution of its reference documents and training materials, several documents contain sensitive information and therefore are distributed through vetted distribution channels.

The Web-based systems that the sector uses to gather and maintain information are developed and implemented to be fully compliant with the DHS cybersecurity certification and accreditation process. This ensures the prevention of intrusions that could compromise the systems and the security of the data that they contain.

Appendix 1: List of Acronyms and Abbreviations

ASDSO	Association of State Dam Safety Officials
ASFPM	Association of State Floodplain Managers
BLM	Bureau of Land Management
BZPP	Buffer Zone Protection Program
CCTV	Closed-Circuit Television
CIKR	Critical Infrastructure and Key Resources
CIP	Critical Infrastructure Protection
CIPAC	Critical Infrastructure Partnership Advisory Council
CSSP	Control Systems Security Program
CTS	Consequence-Based Top-Screen
DCS	Distributed Control Systems
DHS	U.S. Department of Homeland Security
DOE	U.S. Department of Energy
DOI	U.S. Department of the Interior
DOL	U.S. Department of Labor
DSES	Dams Sector Exercise Series
DSPMT	Dam Safety Program Management Tools
DSSP	Dams Sector-Specific Plan
EAP	Emergency Action Plan
EPA	U.S. Environmental Protection Agency
FBI	Federal Bureau of Investigation
FEMA	Federal Emergency Management Agency
FERC	Federal Energy Regulatory Commission
FOIA	Freedom of Information Act
FOUO	For Official Use Only

FWS	Fish and Wildlife Service
GCC	Government Coordinating Council
GHG	Greenhouse Gasses
HAZUS-MH	Hazards U.S.–Multi-Hazard
HITRAC	Homeland Infrastructure Threat and Risk Analysis Center
HSIN	Homeland Security Information Network
HSIN-CS	Homeland Security Information Network–Critical Sectors
HSPD-7	Homeland Security Presidential Directive 7
IBWC	International Boundary and Water Commission
ICODS	Interagency Committee on Dam Safety
ICOLD	International Commission on Large Dams
ICS	Industrial Control Systems
IP	Office of Infrastructure Protection
ISAC	Information Sharing and Analysis Center
ISE	Information-Sharing Environment
IT	Information Technology
LGCC	Levee Sub-Sector Government Coordinating Council
LSCC	Levee Sub-Sector Coordinating Council
NAFSMA	National Association of Flood and Stormwater Management Agencies
NCIP	National Critical Infrastructure Protection
NCSD	National Cybersecurity Division
NDSRB	National Dam Safety Review Board
NERC	North American Electric Reliability Corporation
NICC	National Infrastructure Coordinating Center
NID	National Inventory of Dams
NIPP	National Infrastructure Protection Plan
NIST	National Institute of Standards and Technology
NRCS	Natural Resources Conservation Service
NWS	National Weather Service
OSTP	Office of Science and Technology Policy
PAR	Population at Risk
PCII	Protected Critical Infrastructure Information
PSA	Protective Security Advisor
R&D	Research and Development
RMA	Risk Mitigation Activity

S&T	Science and Technology Directorate
SCADA	Supervisory Control and Data Acquisition
SCC	Sector Coordinating Council
SLTTGCC	State, Local, Tribal, and Territorial Government Coordinating Council
SMA	System of Multiple Assets
SSA	Sector-Specific Agency
SSA EMO	Sector-Specific Agency Executive Management Office
SSP	Sector-Specific Plan
TISP	The Infrastructure Security Partnership
TVA	Tennessee Valley Authority
USACE	U.S. Army Corps of Engineers
US-CERT	United States Computer Emergency Readiness Team
USCG	United States Coast Guard
USDA	U.S. Department of Agriculture
USSD	United States Society on Dams

Appendix 2: Glossary of Terms

Acre-foot. The volume of water that would cover 1 acre to a depth of 1 foot.

All-hazards. A grouping classification encompassing all conditions, environmental or manmade, that have the potential to cause injury, illness, or death; damage to or loss of equipment, infrastructure services, or property; or alternatively causing functional degradation to social, economic, or environmental aspects.

Asset. A person, structure, facility, information, material, or process that has value. In the context of the NIPP, people are not considered assets.

"Black Start" Capabilities. Incremental hydropower available at sites with existing hydroelectric facilities. Incremental hydropower is defined as capacity additions or improved efficiency at existing hydro projects.

Business Continuity. The ability of an organization to continue to function before, during, and after a disaster.

CIKR Partner. Those Federal, State, local, tribal, or territorial governmental entities, public and private sector owners and operators and representative organizations, regional organizations and coalitions, academic and professional entities, and certain not-for-profit and private volunteer organizations that share in the responsibility for protecting the Nation's CIKR.

Consequence. The effect of an event, incident, or occurrence. For the purposes of the NIPP, consequences are divided into four main categories: public health and safety, economic, psychological, and governance impacts. Within the Dams Sector, the focus is on the consequences of the failure of a particular asset and the protective actions that would reduce not only the vulnerability but also the consequences of failure.

Control Systems. Computer-based systems used within many infrastructure and industries to monitor and control sensitive processes and physical functions. These systems typically collect measurement and operational data from the field, process and display the information, and relay control commands to local or remote equipment or human–machine interfaces (operators). Examples of types of control systems include SCADA systems, Process Control Systems, and Distributed Control Systems.

Critical Asset. Dams Sector assets that, if damaged or destroyed, would result in potentially significant consequences, such as loss of life and significant impacts on national economic security, public health and safety, public confidence, or some combination of these adverse outcomes.

Critical Infrastructure. Systems and assets, whether physical or virtual, so vital that the incapacity or destruction of such systems and assets may have a debilitating impact on the security, economy, public health or safety, environment, or any combination of these matters, across any Federal, State, regional, territorial, or local jurisdiction.

Cybersecurity. The prevention of damage to, unauthorized use of, or exploitation of, and, if needed, the restoration of electronic information and communication systems and the information contained therein to ensure confidentiality, integrity, and availability. Includes protection and restoration, when needed, of information networks and wireline, wireless, satellite, public safety answering points, and 911 communication systems and control systems.

Dams. Facilities that include some or all of the following components to perform their intended purposes safely: conventional dam or retaining structure (the structural sections that hold back the water), reservoir (the body of water impounded by the dam), spillways (the structure that passes normal and/or flood flows in a manner that protects the structural integrity of the dam), outlet works (the combination of structures and equipment required for safe operation and control of water released from a reservoir), powerhouse (the structure that houses turbines, generators, and associated control equipment for the production of hydroelectricity), and canal/aqueduct (a constructed channel, usually open, that conveys water by gravity or is used for navigation).

Dependency. The one-directional reliance of an asset, system, network, or collection thereof, within or across sectors, on input, interaction, or other requirement from other sources in order to function properly.

Government Coordinating Council. The government counterpart to the Sector Coordinating Council for each sector established to enable interagency coordination. The GCC comprises representatives across various levels of government (Federal, State, local, tribal, and territorial) as appropriate to the security and operational environment of each individual sector.

Hazard. Natural or manmade source of cause of harm or difficulty.

Incident. An occurrence, caused by either human action or natural phenomena, that may cause harm and may require action. Incidents can include major disasters, emergencies, terrorist attacks, terrorist threats, wild and urban fires, floods, hazardous materials spills, nuclear accidents, aircraft accidents, earthquakes, hurricanes, tornadoes, tropical storms, war-related disasters, public health and medical emergencies, and other occurrences requiring an emergency response.

Infrastructure. The framework of interdependent networks and systems comprising identifiable industries, institutions (including people and procedures), and distribution capabilities that provide a reliable flow of products and services essential to the defense and economic security of the United States, the smooth functioning of government at all levels, and society as a whole. Consistent with the definition in the Homeland Security Act, infrastructure includes physical, cyber, and/or human elements.

Interdependency. Mutually reliant relationship between entities (objects, individuals, or groups) The degree of interdependency does not need to be equal in both directions.

Key Resources. As defined in the Homeland Security Act, key resources are publicly or privately controlled resources essential to the minimal operations of the economy and government.

Levee. Manmade flood protection systems (embankment sections, floodwalls, closure structures, pumps, interior drainage works, and flood damage reduction channels) with the primary purpose of furnishing protection from seasonal high water (floods), storm surges, precipitation, and other weather events.

Lifeline. Important civil works infrastructures such as bridges, pipelines, buildings, and so forth.

Mitigation. Ongoing and sustained action to reduce the probability of or lessen the impact of an adverse incident.

Network. A group of components that share information or interact with each other in order to perform a function.

Normalize. In the context of the NIPP, the process of transforming risk-related data into comparable units.

Owners/Operators. Those entities responsible for day-to-day operations and investment in a particular asset or system.

Preparedness. The activities necessary to build, sustain, and improve readiness capabilities to prevent, protect against, respond to, and recover from natural or manmade incidents. Preparedness is a continuous process involving efforts at all levels of government and between government and the private sector and nongovernmental organizations to identify threats, determine vulnerabilities, and identify the required resources to prevent, respond to, and recover from major incidents.

Prevention. Actions taken and measures put in place for the continual assessment and readiness of necessary actions to reduce the risk of threats and vulnerabilities, to intervene and stop an occurrence, or to mitigate effects.

Prioritization. In the context of the NIPP, prioritization is the process of using risk assessment results to identify where risk reduction or mitigation efforts are most needed and subsequently determine which protective actions should be instituted in order to have the greatest effect.

Protected Critical Infrastructure Information (PCII). PCII refers to all critical infrastructure information, including categorical inclusion PCII, that has undergone the validation process and that the PCII Program Office has determined qualifies for protection under the Critical Infrastructure Information Act. All information submitted to the PCII Program Office or designee with an express statement is presumed to be PCII until the PCII Program Office determines otherwise.

Protection. The actions or measures taken to cover or shield from exposure, injury, or destruction. In the context of the NIPP, protection includes actions to deter the threat, mitigate the vulnerabilities, or minimize the consequences associated with a terrorist attack, natural hazards or other incidents. Protection can include a wide range of activities, such as hardening facilities, building resilience and redundancy, incorporating hazard resistance into initial facility design, initiating active or passive countermeasures, installing security systems, promoting workforce surety, training and exercises, and implementing cybersecurity measures, among various others.

Protective Program. A set of measures designed to prevent, detect, deter, and mitigate the threat; reduce vulnerability to an attack or other disaster; minimize consequences; and enable timely, efficient response and restoration in a post-event situation, whether a terrorist attack, natural disaster, or other incident.

Recovery. The development, coordination, and execution of service- and site-restoration plans for affected communities and the reconstitution of government operations and services through individual, private sector, nongovernmental, and public assistance programs that identify needs and define resources; provide housing and promote restoration; address long-term care and treatment of affected persons; implement additional measures for community restoration; incorporate mitigation measures and techniques, as feasible; evaluate the incident to identify lessons learned; and develop initiatives to mitigate the effects of future incidents.

Resilience. The ability to resist, absorb, recover from, or successfully adapt to adversity or a change in conditions.

Response. Activities that address the short-term, direct effects of an incident, including immediate actions to save lives, protect property, and meet basic human needs. Response also includes the execution of emergency operations plans and incident mitigation activities designed to limit the loss of life, personal injury, property damage, and other unfavorable outcomes. As indicated by the situation, response activities include applying intelligence and other information to lessen the effects or consequences of an incident; increased security operations; continuing investigations into the nature and source of the threat; ongoing surveillance and testing processes; immunizations, isolation, or quarantine; and specific law enforcement operations aimed at preempting, interdicting, or disrupting illegal activity, and apprehending actual perpetrators and bringing them to justice.

Risk. The potential for an unwanted outcome resulting from an incident, event, or occurrence, as determined by its likelihood and the associated consequences.

Risk-Informed Decisionmaking. The determination of a course of action predicated on the assessment of risk, the expected impact of that course of action on that risk, and other relevant factors.

Risk Management Framework. A planning methodology that outlines the process for setting security goals; identifying assets, systems, networks, and functions; assessing risks; prioritizing and implementing protective programs; measuring performance; and taking corrective action. Public and private sector entities often include risk management frameworks in their business continuity plans.

Sector. A logical collection of assets, systems, or networks that provide a common function to the economy, government, or society. The NIPP addresses 18 CIKR sectors under the authority provided by HSPD-7.

Sector Assets. The assets, systems, and networks related to dam projects, navigation locks, levees, hurricane barriers, mine tailings and other industrial impoundments, or other similar water retention and/or control facilities.

Sector Coordinating Council. The private sector counterpart to the GCCs, these councils are self-organized, self-run, and self-governed organizations that are representative of a spectrum of key stakeholders within a sector. SCCs serve as the government's principal point of entry into each sector for developing and coordinating a wide range of CIKR protection activities and issues.

Sector Partnership Model. The framework used to promote and facilitate sector and cross-sector planning, coordination, collaboration, and information sharing for CIKR protection involving all levels of government and private sector entities.

Sector-Specific Agency. Federal departments and agencies identified in HSPD-7 as responsible for CIKR protection activities in specified CIKR sectors.

Sector-Specific Plan. Augmenting plans that complement and extend the NIPP Base Plan and detail the application of the NIPP framework specific to each CIKR sector. The SSPs are developed by the SSAs in close collaboration with other sector partners.

System. Any combination of facilities, equipment, personnel, procedures, and communications integrated for a specific purpose.

Terrorism. Premeditated threat or act of violence against noncombatant persons, property, or environmental or economic targets to induce fear, intimidate, coerce, or affect a government, the civilian population, or any segment thereof, in furtherance of political, social, ideological, or religious objectives.

Threat. A natural or manmade occurrence, individual, entity, or action that has or indicates the potential to harm life, information, operations, the environment, and/or property.

Value Proposition. A statement that outlines the national and homeland security interest in protecting the Nation's CIKR and articulates the benefits gained by all CIKR partners through the risk management framework and public-private partnership described in the NIPP.

Vulnerability. A physical feature or operational attribute that renders an entity open to exploitation or susceptible to a given hazard.

Appendix 3: Information Security Framework

Cybersecurity guidelines, such as those specified by the National Institute of Standards and Technology (NIST) in NIST Special Publication (SP) 800-53, *Recommended Security Controls for Federal Information Systems*, and NIST SP 800-82, *Guide to Industrial Control Systems Security*, generally offer more granularity in the context of defining an electronic security perimeter around industrial control systems (ICS) assets. NIST SP 800-53 was originally developed to apply to traditional government-operated information technology (IT) systems and contains specifications for information security controls that are binding for all non-national security information and information systems belonging to, or operated for, Federal agencies.

As part of the ongoing initiative to develop a unified information security framework for the Federal Government and its contractors, NIST SP 800-53 revision 3 includes security controls for both national security and non-national security systems. The updated security control catalog incorporates best practices in information security from the U.S. Department of Defense, the intelligence community, and civil agencies to produce the most broad-based and comprehensive set of safeguards and countermeasures ever developed for information systems. The standardized set of management, operational, and technical controls provides a common specification language for information security for Federal information systems processing, storing, and transmitting national security and non-national security information. The revised security control catalog also includes the state-of-the-practice safeguards and countermeasures needed by organizations to address advanced cyber threats capable of exploiting vulnerabilities in Federal information and ICS. In 2006, NIST also established the Industrial Control System Security Project to improve the security of public and private sector ICS; a major part of the project is to research the applicability of SP 800-53 to ICS and to clarify/rectify any problems in its application.

NIST standards are mandatory for Federal facilities under the Federal Information Security Management Act (FISMA), enacted in 2002 as Title III of the E-Government Act of 2002. The act recognizes the importance of information security to the economic and national security interests of the United States. The act requires each Federal agency to develop, document, and implement an agency-wide program to provide information security for information and information systems.

Appendix 4: Dams Sector Authorities

Asset owners and operators are responsible for the safety and security of their assets and for their maintenance, upgrade, and repair. Asset safety and security often are not solely Federal, State, or local issues because an incident can affect persons and property across local, State, and even national borders. An incident involving an asset in one area can affect commerce, navigation, and power generation and distribution, or it can cause severe damage in another area.

Key authorities that govern and/or have a general influence on the Dams Sector are summarized below:

Federal Power Act of 1920: Authorizes the Federal Energy Regulatory Commission (FERC) to regulate hydroelectric projects, including dams, reservoirs, and other projects to enhance navigation and power generation. The act authorizes FERC to regulate and license the construction, operation, and maintenance of dams, reservoirs, power terminals, and other structures designed to improve navigation and transmission of power by way of navigable waterways.

Tennessee Valley Authority (TVA) Act of 1933: Established the TVA and gave it the powers and duties for projects in the Tennessee Valley Region, such as flood control; maintenance of navigational waters; management of water quality; dam safety; economic development; and acquisition of real estate for the construction of dams, reservoirs, transmission lines, powerhouses, and other structures.

Flood Control Act of 1936: Placed watersheds, waterflow retardation, and soil erosion prevention under the U.S. Department of Agriculture and authorized the U.S. Army Corps of Engineers (USACE) to undertake civil engineering projects such as dams, levees, dikes, and other flood control measures for the improvement of rivers and other waterways for flood control and allied purposes. Those authorities were not to interfere with reclamation projects by the U.S. Department of the Interior's Bureau of Reclamation. The Flood Control Act of 1928 authorized USACE to design and construct projects for the control of floods on the Mississippi River and its tributaries, as well as the Sacramento River in California.

Federal Mine Safety and Health Act of 1977: This act amended the Federal Coal Mine Health and Safety Act of 1969 to encompass all mines under a single legislation—surface and underground—regardless of size, commodity mined, or method of extraction. The act requires that the Mine Safety and Health Administration inspect all mines each year. Underground mines are to receive at least four inspections annually; all surface operations are to be inspected at least twice annually. Advance notice of inspections is prohibited. The act requires or authorizes additional inspections and investigations to ensure safe and healthy work environments for miners. Violations found during inspections and investigations must be cited and are subject to civil penalties. Mine operators must notify the Mine Safety and Health Administration when they open or close a mine.

Dam Safety Act of 2006: Reauthorized the National Dam Safety Program through Fiscal Year 2011 and continues all of the programs established by the 1996 act and the 2002 reauthorization that increase the safety of the Nation's dams. These programs include grants to the States for the improvement of State dam safety programs, training for State dam safety staff and inspectors, a program of technical and archival research, and funding to USACE for maintaining and updating the National Inventory of

Dams. The 2006 act also continued the role of the National Dam Safety Review Board, which provides the Administrator of the Federal Emergency Management Agency with advice on national policy issues affecting dam safety.

Water Resources Development Act of 2007: Subtitle C, National Levee Safety Program, directs the Secretary of the Army to establish a National Levee Safety Committee to (1) advise the Secretary in implementing a national levee safety program; (2) support programs, policies, and guidelines to enhance levee safety for the protection of human life and property throughout the United States; and (3) support coordination and information exchange between Federal and State agencies that share common problems and responsibilities related to levee safety. The Secretary is also directed to establish and maintain a national levee safety program, which shall include (1) periodically publishing an inventory of levees in the United States, including assessment and inspection results; (2) determining the potential for a failure or overtopping of each levee in the United States that would pose a risk to human life or public safety, with priority going to levees that constitute the highest risk; and (3) taking into consideration the potential of a levee to fail or overtop because of hydrologic or hydraulic conditions; storm surges; geotechnical conditions; inadequate operating procedures; structural, mechanical, or design deficiencies; or other conditions in the vicinity of the levee. The act sets forth provisions regarding state participation, reporting requirements, and subsequent assessments.

Key authorities that govern and/or have an influence on the Dams Sector's approach to infrastructure protection are as follows:

Critical Infrastructure Information Act of 2002: Enacted as part of the Homeland Security Act, this act creates a framework that enables members of the private sector and others to voluntarily submit sensitive information regarding the Nation's critical infrastructure and key resources (CIKR) to the U.S. Department of Homeland Security (DHS) with the assurance that the information, if it satisfies certain requirements, will be protected from public disclosure. The Protected Critical Infrastructure Information (PCII) Program, created under the authority of this act, is central to the NIPP's information-sharing and protection strategy. By protecting sensitive information submitted through the program, the private sector is assured that the information will remain secure and will be used only to further CIKR protection efforts.

Federal Information Security Management Act of 2002 (FISMA): Enacted as Title III of the E-Government Act, FISMA requires each Federal agency to develop, document, and implement an agency-wide program to provide information security for the information and information systems that support the operations and assets of the agency, including those provided or managed by another agency, contractor, or other source.

Homeland Security Act of 2002: Establishes a Cabinet-level department headed by a Secretary of Homeland Security with the mandate and legal authority to protect the American people from the continuing threat of terrorism. The mission of DHS is to prevent terrorist attacks within the United States, reduce the vulnerability of the United States to terrorism at home, minimize the damage and assist in the recovery from terrorist attacks that occur, and ensure that the overall economic security of the United States is not diminished by the efforts, activities, and programs aimed at securing the homeland. To fulfill another mission—protection of the Nation's CIKR—DHS is to complete comprehensive assessments of CIKR vulnerabilities, including the performance of risk assessments to determine the risks posed by particular types of terrorist attacks; develop a comprehensive national plan for securing CIKR and the physical and technological assets that support such systems; and recommend, in coordination with other agencies of the Federal Government and in cooperation with State and local government agencies and authorities, the private sector, and other entities, the measures necessary to protect CIKR. These requirements, combined with the President's direction in HSPD-7, mandate the unified approach to CIKR protection taken in the NIPP.

Homeland Security Presidential Directive 7 (HSPD-7), Critical Infrastructure Identification, Prioritization, and Protection, 2003: Establishes a framework for Federal departments and agencies to identify, prioritize, and protect CIKR from terrorist attacks, with an emphasis on protecting against catastrophic health effects and mass casualties. This directive establishes a national policy for Federal departments and agencies to identify and prioritize the Nation's CIKR and to protect it from terrorist attacks. HSPD-7 mandates the creation and implementation of the NIPP and sets forth roles and responsibilities for DHS; the SSAs; other Federal departments and agencies; and State, local, tribal, private sector, and other sector partners.

There are no nationwide authorities governing levees, nor any overarching nationwide levee safety program. For projects that are owned and operated by USACE, operations and maintenance are managed through the Operations and Maintenance Budget Process. For projects built by USACE and operated and maintained by a local sponsor, the USACE authority is only to periodically inspect the sponsor's compliance in performing the required operation and maintenance. Some State governments have initiated various activities to regulate and/or inventory levees within their State boundaries.

Appendix 5: Facility-Specific Assessments

Relevant physical, cyber, and human elements associated with assessments at the facility level are described below:

Physical Security Systems Assessment. The purpose of a physical security assessment is to evaluate the physical security systems in place or planned, and to identify vulnerabilities and potential physical security improvements for the sites being evaluated. Physical security systems include access controls, barriers, locks and keys, badges and passes, intrusion detection devices and associated alarm reporting and display, closed-circuit television, communications equipment, interior and exterior lighting, power sources, inventory control, signs and postings, security system wiring, and protective forces. The physical security systems are reviewed for their design, installation, operation, and maintenance, and are tested.

Physical Asset Analysis. The purpose of physical asset analysis is to examine systems and physical operational assets. This examination includes asset utilization, system redundancies, and emergency operating procedures. It looks specifically for those elements that, either solely or in concert with other factors, provide a high potential for disruption of service or unacceptable consequences.

Operations Security Assessment. Operations security is the process of denying potential adversaries information about the capabilities, vulnerabilities, and intentions of the owning organization. This denial of information is accomplished by identifying, controlling, and protecting information and activities that are of a sensitive nature. The vulnerability assessment should include a review of security training and awareness programs, as well as information that may be available through public access.

Analysis of Policies and Procedures. Security policies and procedures provide the basis for identifying and resolving issues, and are the foundation of day-to-day security operations. Policies and procedures should be reviewed to ensure that they address key factors affecting security, enable effective implementation and enforcement, conform to established standards and guidance, and address roles and responsibilities.

Characterization of the Threat Environment. Developing a clear understanding of threats is a fundamental element of vulnerability assessments and risk management. Threats, threat trends, tactics, and motivations should be characterized. To the extent possible, characterization of the threat environment should be localized to the facility area.

Cybersecurity Assessment. This review provides an analysis of the security features of the facility's cyber infrastructure. A thorough review should cover the following 10 topic areas: (1) cybersecurity policy, (2) electronic access control, (3) personnel security, (4) physical and environmental security, (5) cybersecurity awareness and training, (6) monitoring and incident response, (7) disaster recovery and business continuity, (8) systems development and acquisition, (9) configuration management, and (10) risk (and vulnerability) management.

Examples of security assessment approaches that are relevant to the Dams Sector are provided below:

Risk Assessment Methodology for Dams (RAM-D^{SM}): Developed by Sandia National Laboratories under the auspices of the Interagency Forum on Infrastructure Protection (IFIP). IFIP was chartered in 1997 as a forum in which to exchange security and protection system information among owners and operators of Federal dams and related infrastructure. Members of IFIP include the USACE, the Bureau of Reclamation, the TVA, the Bonneville Power Administration, the Western Area Power Administration, the Federal Bureau of Investigation, the U.S. Department of Energy, and Sandia National Laboratories. The methodology is an adaptation of the security principles and procedures developed to protect nuclear facilities. The approach provides procedures for completing threat and consequence assessments, a systematic process for determining the effectiveness of security systems, and mechanisms to evaluate the relative level of risk and the need for security upgrades or consequence mitigation measures for risk reduction.

Dam Assessment Matrix for Security and Vulnerability Risk (DAMSVR): Developed by Security Management Solutions and the Federal Energy Regulatory Commission with expertise and technical assistance provided by the Bureau of Reclamation, the USACE, and representatives of the Association of State Dam Safety Officials. The DAMSVR approach is an adaptation of the CARVER (Criticality, Accessibility, Recuperability, Vulnerability, Effect, Recognizability) method and provides a systematic methodology to determine relative risk scores for assets or project features by considering identified vulnerabilities, threats, and mitigation measures. DAMSVR is distributed by the Federal Energy Regulatory Commission.

Critical Asset and Portfolio Risk Analysis (CAPRA): Developed by the University of Maryland, this quantitative approach is suited for all-hazards risk analysis. The approach includes the following phases: scenario identification, consequence and criticality assessment, security vulnerability assessment, hazard likelihood assessment, and cost-benefit analysis. CAPRA provides a systematic approach to evaluate relevant hazard scenarios and identify representative attack profiles considering alternative delivery systems and intrusion paths. The methodology considers physical (fragility, mitigation effectiveness, and response effectiveness) and security (probability of detection, delay time, response time, and probability of neutralization) vulnerabilities. The probability of attack for each attack profile is estimated based on relative attractiveness. The methodology produces actionable risk assessments and facilitates quantitative cost-benefit analysis. All values (risk, cost, and benefit) are expressed in dollars per year, and thus the cost-benefit ratio gives a measure of the number of dollars realized in benefit for each dollar spent on risk reduction.

Maritime Security Risk Analysis Model (MSRAM): Developed by U.S. Coast Guard (USCG), MSRAM is a tool that provides decisionmakers at various levels with actionable information regarding the risk to critical infrastructure in the maritime domain, including the Nation's navigable waterways. MSRAM allows decisionmakers to understand the geographic density of risk across the Nation's ports, know the profile of risk within a port, and recognize asset-specific risks. The methodology considers the risk posed by different scenarios in terms of threat, vulnerability, and consequence. MSRAM considers area-wide security measures and response capabilities and it is designed to capture the security risk facing different types of targets spanning every sector within the maritime domain, allowing comparison among different targets and geographic areas.

Cyber Security Evaluation Tool (CSET): Developed by the National Cybersecurity Division with assistance from the NIST, CSET is a desktop software tool that provides users with a systematic and repeatable approach for assessing the security posture of cyber systems and networks against recognized industry standards. The output from CSET is a prioritized list of recommendations for improving the cybersecurity posture of an organization's enterprise and industrial control cyber systems. The tool derives the recommendations from a database of cybersecurity standards, guidelines, and practices.

Other approaches and methodologies specifically relevant to power generation facilities include the following:

- **American Electric Power Method:** Uses an attack tree approach to identify and characterize risks.
- **Australia/New Zealand Risk Management Guideline (AS/NZS 4360, 2004):** Provides general risk assessment and management guidance.

- **Continual Risk Management:** Developed by Veridian Security Analysis; used by some organizations to develop risk assessments for numerous assets of critical energy infrastructure.

- **U.S. Department of Energy's Vulnerability and Risk Assessment Program:** Focuses generically on vulnerability assessments.

- **Edison Electric Institute Security Committee Approach to Risk/Vulnerability Assessment:** A fairly straightforward, non-empirical assessment method that assists asset owners in determining risk by first identifying the vulnerabilities and available mitigation measures and consequences of the loss of key assets and subsequently assessing overall risk on the basis of that analysis.

- **Electric Power Research Institute Security Vulnerability Self-Assessment Guidelines for the Electric Power Industry:** Provides guidance, templates, and checklists to assess security vulnerability.

- **Pacific Gas and Electric Vulnerability Assessment Checklist Approach:** Provides a straightforward system for ensuring that all aspects of the individual dam facility are included in a vulnerability analysis.

- **Pacific Northwest National Laboratory's Communication Assessment Prioritization Program:** Provides qualitative and semi-quantitative tools that can be adapted for evaluating security risks.

Appendix 6: Facility-Specific Protective Measures

The process that can be used to develop and implement facility-specific protective measures is described below. Given the programs currently in place and those being developed, the identification of protective needs is driven by two factors: the potential threat and the risk presented to a given facility. Responding to needs requires identifying the constraints associated with the need and then developing protective actions to address them.

The process for developing appropriate protective measures typically will consist of, at a minimum, the following four steps.

1. **Characterize the potential threat:** Characterizing the potential threat provides the required parameters for designers of protective programs and resilience strategies and aids them in identifying and selecting appropriate protective measures. For manmade incidents, identification of potential threats should be based on a complete analysis of plausible targets, tactics, tools, weapons, and explosives. In addition to the characterization of the set of potential threats, the analysis should include a quantification of their relative likelihood.

2. **Determine the appropriate level of protection:** The level of protection refers to the degree of an asset's protection against a given threat based on the asset's value to its owner and users. The level of protection can relate to the tolerable level of risk. A low amount of tolerated damage equates to a high level of protection, which corresponds to a low possibility that an asset will be compromised if attacked. The level of protection also can refer to the probability that an aggressor will be defeated before the asset is compromised. A high probability of defeating an adversary corresponds to a high level of protection.

3. **Identify constraints:** Potential solutions to a given threat might be limited to rapid recovery or mitigation measures to prevent or limit the consequences if defensive measures are not available, would be prohibitively expensive, could not be implemented in an effective time frame, or conflict with project operations. Constraints may be governed by the physical characteristics of the facility or by operational considerations that may restrict the nature of asset-specific security measures. During development of the protective program, nontechnical constraints are considered in relation to user requirements.

4. **Design and implement protective measures:** The general strategy for protecting critical physical and cyber assets includes measures for detection, delay, assessment, response, redundancy, and recovery:

Detection. Because detection often is achieved through electronic devices, it is independent of utilizing people as a means of alarm or annunciation.

Delay. Delay does not begin until detection has occurred. Delay typically is achieved through site measures such as increasing the distance between an asset and the sensored perimeter, or installing hardening features.

Assessment. Assessment typically consists of a person or persons evaluating security systems in place.

Response. Response involves an appropriately trained and armed response force arriving at the asset and intervening and preventing its compromise, thus preventing an undesirable event from occurring.

Redundancy. Redundancy involves a means for providing similar benefits to users in the event that an asset is destroyed or its operational capability is reduced. Redundancy is thus a form of mitigation. Mitigation and recovery operations benefit from redundancy at a critical project asset or at the critical project.

Recovery. Recovery typically refers to actions taken to reestablish the asset's function after an undesirable event has occurred. Recovery plans may be developed for a particular asset or set of assets. Recovery plans are valuable because they are applicable to all threats (as well as normal deterioration) and are transferable to different infrastructure sites. They can limit the impact from the loss of an asset and cost much less than physical or operational protective measures.

Appendix 7: Connections with Other Sectors

The Energy Sector

The Energy Sector comprises thousands of assets related to three key energy resources: electric power, petroleum, and natural gas. The assets are geographically dispersed but connected by systems and networks; more than 85 percent of the country's energy infrastructure is owned by the private sector.

The electricity segment of the Energy Sector contains more than 5,300 power plants with approximately 1,075 gigawatts of installed generating capacity. Approximately 49 percent of electricity is produced by combusting coal (primarily transported by rail), 19 percent in nuclear power plants, and 20 percent by combusting natural gas. Hydroelectric plants contribute 7 percent of the Nation's electricity. Oil is used to produce 2 percent and 3 percent is developed through renewable (solar, wind, and geothermal) and other sources.

Electricity generated at power plants is transmitted over 211,000 miles of high-voltage transmission lines. Voltage is stepped down at substations before being distributed to 140 million customers over millions of miles of lower voltage distribution lines. The electricity infrastructure is highly automated and controlled by utilities and regional grid operators using sophisticated energy management systems that are supplied by supervisory control and data acquisition (SCADA) systems to keep the system in balance.

The Energy Sector's petroleum segment entails the exploration, production, storage, transport, and refinement of crude oil. The crude oil is refined into petroleum products which are then stored and distributed to key economic sectors throughout the United States. Key petroleum products include motor gasoline, jet fuel, distillate fuel oil, residual fuel oil, and liquefied petroleum gases.

Both crude oil and petroleum products are imported, primarily by ship, as well as produced domestically. Currently, 66 percent of the crude oil required to fuel the U.S. economy is imported. In the United States, there are more than 500,000 crude oil-producing wells, 30,000 miles of gathering pipeline, and 51,000 miles of crude oil pipeline. There are 133 operable petroleum refineries, 116,000 miles of product pipeline, and 1,400 petroleum terminals. Petroleum also relies on sophisticated SCADA and other systems to control production and distribution; however, crude oil and petroleum products are stored in tank farms and other facilities.

Natural gas is also produced, piped, stored, and distributed in the United States. Imports of liquefied natural gas (LNG) are increasing to meet growing demand. There are more than 448,000 gas production and condensate wells and 20,000 miles of gathering pipeline in the country. Gas is processed (impurities removed) at more than 550 operable gas processing plants and there are almost 302,000 miles of interstate and intrastate pipeline for the transmission of natural gas. Gas is stored at 399 underground storage fields and 103 LNG peaking facilities. Finally, natural gas is distributed to homes and businesses over 1,175,000 miles of distribution pipelines.

The U.S. Department of Energy is the Sector-Specific Agency for the Energy Sector.

The Water Sector

The Water Sector, which comprises drinking water and wastewater assets, has a long history of implementing programs to provide clean and safe water, thereby protecting public health and the environment across the Nation.

There are approximately 153,000 public water systems (PWSs) in the United States. The U.S. Environmental Protection Agency (EPA) classifies these water systems according to the number of people that they serve, the source of their water, and whether they serve the same customers year-round or on an occasional basis. PWSs provide water for human consumption through pipes or other constructed conveyances to at least 15 service connections or serve an average of at least 25 people for at least 60 days per year.

EPA has defined three types of PWSs:

1. A community water system (CWS) is a PWS that supplies water to the same population year-round.

2. A non-transient, non-community water system (NTNCWS) is a PWS that regularly supplies water to at least 25 of the same people at least 6 months per year, but not year-round. Some examples are schools, factories, office buildings, and hospitals that have their own water systems.

3. A transient, non-community water system (TNCWS) is a PWS that provides water in a place such as a gas station or campground where people do not remain for long periods of time.

There are more than 51,000 CWSs, more than 18,000 NTNCWSs, and approximately 84,000 TNCWSs in the United States. Of the CWS, 42,624 (82 percent) are small or very small systems serving 30 percent of the population who get their water from a CWS and 9,027 systems (18 percent) are very large, large, or medium systems serving 70 percent of the population who get their water from a CWS.

The Water Sector also includes more than 16,000 publicly owned wastewater treatment systems. The majority of the U.S. population has its sanitary sewerage treated by these wastewater systems. Most wastewater is treated by publicly owned treatment works (POTWs), although there are a small number of private facilities such as industrial plants. The POTWs and privately owned wastewater treatment works that discharge treated effluent into the waters of the United States are subject to regulation under the National Pollutant Discharge Elimination System (NPDES) program, either through the State or EPA.

Typical POTWs include a network of pipes that conveys wastewater from the source to the treatment plant. In some older cities, the wastewater and stormwater collection systems are integrated into combined sewer systems and, in wet weather, the combined effluent may be discharged directly to the receiving body, bypassing the treatment plant. Tanks or impoundments are used to store raw sewage and industrial effluent, generally for the purposes of flow equalization, prior to treatment through a variety of physical, biological, and chemical treatment processes applied to plant influent to reduce pollutant levels to the concentrations specified in the NPDES permit in the case of a direct discharger or other specified discharge. Lagoons hold treated wastewater prior to its discharge to a surface water body. Monitoring and SCADA systems may also be in place.

EPA is the SSA for the Water Sector. The agency has a longstanding tradition of working through its 10 regional offices and with the 50 States, the District of Columbia, tribes, and 6 Territories on oversight and implementation of regulations pertaining to assets within the Water Sector.

The Transportation Systems Sector: The Maritime Transportation System

The Transportation Systems Sector consists of six key subsectors (modes) that quickly, safely, and securely move people and goods through the United States and internationally: Aviation, Highway, Maritime Transportation System, Mass Transit, Pipeline Systems, and Rail. The Maritime Transportation System (MTS) is the mode most closely interconnected with the Dams Sector. The MTS is complex and geographically and physically diverse in character and operation. Ninety-nine percent of overseas trade by volume enters or leaves the United States by ship. In 2008, approximately 7,119 oceangoing vessels made 60,578 calls at U.S. ports; these ports accounted for approximately 8 percent of global vessel calls. In that same year, U.S. waterborne trades (foreign and domestic) totaled 2.3 billion metric tons and 64 million passenger-nights were booked on North American cruises.

The maritime domain of the United States consists of more than 95,000 miles of coastline, 360 ports, 3.4 million square miles of Exclusive Economic Zones, and 25,000 miles of navigable waterways. The Nation's navigable waterways are extensive and include coastal and ocean areas, including the Great Lakes St. Lawrence Seaway System; the Mississippi, Ohio, and Columbia River systems; canals; the Atlantic and Gulf Intracoastal Waterways; and Arctic waterways. They serve as waterways to transport manufactured, mineral, agricultural, and bulk products; other trade goods; and passengers to and within America, and are used for commercial, recreational, scientific, and military purposes. Navigation on the Maritime Transportation System is supported and facilitated by a system of canals, locks, dams, and aids to navigation. The system includes 236 lock chambers at 192 lock sites owned and/or operated by USACE, and more than 3,700 marine terminals and 1,400 intermodal connections.

USCG is the SSA for the Maritime Mode. The Transportation Security Administration (TSA) is the SSA for the remaining modes of the Transportation Systems Sector. USCG works collaboratively with TSA and other Federal, State, local, and tribal entities as the chair of the Maritime Modal Government Coordinating Council. USCG also works with industry partners to help prevent, prepare for, protect against, respond to, and recover from transportation security incidents, natural disasters, and other emergencies. Other security partnerships include international cooperation vis-à-vis participation in international organizations and other multilateral and bilateral forums and exchanges.

Appendix 8: Sector-Specific Agency Executive Management Office

DHS is the SSA for 11 of the 18 CIKR sectors. The Secretary of Homeland Security designated the Office of Infrastructure Protection (IP) to carry out the SSA mission for six of those CIKR sectors: the Chemical, Commercial Facilities, Critical Manufacturing, Dams, Emergency Services, and Nuclear Sectors.

As a component of the DHS National Protection and Programs Directorate, IP is responsible for managing the coordinated national program to reduce all-hazards risk to the Nation's CIKR and for strengthening national preparedness, timely response, and rapid recovery in the event of an incident or emergency. IP manages this broad mission through three broad program areas:

- Identifying and analyzing threats and vulnerabilities;
- Coordinating nationally and locally through partnerships with both government and private sector entities that share information and resources; and
- Mitigating risk and effects (encompassing both readiness and incident response).

IP created the Sector-Specific Agency Executive Management Office (SSA EMO) to oversee the SSA Management Project and to implement the mission of leading the unified public-private sector effort to coordinate, develop, and implement a comprehensive security strategy for the six CIKR sectors for which it is responsible. Each branch chief (e.g., Dams, Nuclear, etc.) within the SSA EMO must effectively carry out numerous functions that overlap with and are dependent on other IP projects and activities.

To execute its mission, the SSA EMO established five primary program areas that support implementation of the SSPs: planning and project integration, education and training, partnership and information sharing, exercises and incident management, and assessment and mitigation. These program areas contain cross-sector and sector-specific initiatives that allow the SSA EMO to manage the overall process for building security partnerships and for implementing the Sector-Specific Plan (SSP) by leveraging CIKR security expertise, relationships, and resource investments that are prioritized on the basis of effective risk management.

The efficiencies created by grouping the six sectors under one organizational structure ensure that each SSA EMO sector is able to carry out its responsibilities to lead, coordinate, and implement its SSP in partnership with its public and private sector stakeholders, and provide sector-specific input for the ongoing implementation of the overarching national cross-sector CIKR strategy.